# THE MOST INCREDIBLE HOCKEY STORIES EVER TOLD

INSPIRATIONAL AND LEGENDARY TALES
FROM THE GREATEST HOCKEY PLAYERS
AND GAMES OF ALL TIME

**Hank Patton**

ISBN: 979-8-89095-018-5

# CONTENTS

# ATTENTION:

DO YOU WANT MY FUTURE BOOKS AT
HEAVY DISCOUNTS AND EVEN FOR FREE?

HEAD OVER TO WWW.SECRETREADS.COM
AND JOIN MY SECRET BOOK CLUB!

# INTRODUCTION

Ice hockey is one of the least understood sports by many people around the world as it is sometimes considered difficult to access. It is expensive, and the rules can often be confusing, especially since they rely on a small rubber disc that moves faster than can be seen on a television. Because of these limitations, many potential fans struggle to understand the spectacle that is the game of ice hockey.

Players from both teams fly around the ice surface on their skates, making quick passes and using their bodies to punish their opponents, all while trying to get the puck to pass by a goaltender brave enough to stand in the way.

It is a glorious, brutal game. Because of the different skills required to play the game, hockey players are considered to be some of the best-rounded athletes in the world. When players of this caliber are brought together in one league, to compete with and against each other, incredible moments are bound to happen. This book seeks to deliver some of those incredible moments to you.

In these pages, you'll learn about some of the best players, teams, and moments to ever happen in the sport. From some of the best women to ever lace up the skates, to the college play that became a sensation around the world, this book will explore the very best that ice hockey has to offer.

We'll look at players who revolutionized how the game is played and those who simply dominated the sport for decades on end. After all, although hockey is a team sport, individuals have made themselves known on an international level with their talents, putting them a cut above the rest of the best.

Their stories will show you that their skill on the ice would be nothing without determination, grit, and a bottomless well of effort. If you've ever skated before, and fallen hard onto the ice, you'll know that getting up is much more difficult than standing up in a field of grass, clay, or the wooden flooring of a basketball court. These players, teams, and moments are more than just special. The accomplishments in these pages are simply incredible.

# CHAPTER 1:

## THE CAREER OF TIM THOMAS

The career of a goaltender, compared to that of any other playing position in the sport, is the narrowest path. Teams dress only two goalies per game, compared to triple the number of defensemen and six times as many forwards. Simply put, there are fewer opportunities for a goaltender to make it all the way to the NHL.

Most goalies who do make the trek do so through minor leagues. They are often drafted in their late teens or early twenties, and they begin their NHL careers by the age of 24 or 25. However, there are rare exceptions when goaltenders have a bit more journeying before they reach the big league, but those goalies are rarely big-impact players. Tim Thomas is one of the few exceptions.

Let's look at the incredible career of Timothy Thomas Jnr.

After playing high school hockey at Davison High School in Michigan, Tim Thomas excelled at college hockey at the University of Vermont. During his four years at the school, he helped the team to 81 wins against 43 losses and 15 ties. He personally posted a .934 save percentage, which is excellent. He was part of a team that made their first Frozen Four in 1996. To this day, Thomas leads the school in games played as a goaltender, wins, and total saves.

Thomas was drafted 217th in the 1994 draft by the Quebec Nordiques, which was during his sophomore year of college, but he did not make the jump to the NHL. Instead, after finishing his college career, he moved to a couple of different minor-league teams. Specifically, Thomas had very quick stints with the Birmingham Bulls of the East Coast Hockey League, as well as the Houston Aeros of the International Hockey League, before he moved to Europe to play for HIFK of the SM-Liga, the professional league in Finland.

During his time in Finland, he played 18 games with an impressive .947 save percentage as his team won the Finnish championship. That summer, Thomas attracted attention from NHL teams again, and he signed with the Edmonton Oilers. He was then assigned to the Oilers' minor league team, the Hamilton Bulldogs. He played in only 15 games before going back to Finland to finish another season there.

Thomas continued his back-and-forth career by returning to the United States in 1999 to play for the Detroit Vipers, and while he played 36 games there, his numbers were not impressive. Once again, the following year, he moved back to Europe, but this time to Sweden, where he played for AIK for one season.

His performance in Sweden was above average, with a .918 save percentage in 43 regular season games, but he still couldn't stay put.

At this point in his career, after four years and seven different moves between teams and leagues, one might expect Tim Thomas to become a journeyman of sorts or a veteran of the minor leagues. Everyone knows players like this, who are so close to making it to an NHL roster but can never get over the hump.

Still, Thomas continued grinding away and working on his game. After his season in Sweden, he once again moved to Finland, this time with Karpat, where his save percentage improved slightly, up to .925. Finally, another NHL team was ready to take a gamble with the goaltender, but this time it was the Boston Bruins.

In the 2002–2003 season, Thomas played for the Bruins' minor league team in Providence, and he also got the call to play in four regular season games for the NHL squad. His numbers were great, but he was still lower on the depth chart. But, for the first time, he stayed put during the offseason and played for Providence during the 2003–2004 season, posting an amazing .941 save percentage.

Things were looking promising for Thomas at this point. He didn't get called up to play for Boston during that second season, but his performances were fantastic, and he was making an impression on the management of the team.

However, as fate would have it, the NHL was not quite ready for Tim Thomas, or for any hockey at all. The 2004–2005 NHL season was canceled entirely because players and management could not agree on salary cap rules.

Of course, instead of sitting around and waiting for the NHL to come back, Tim Thomas returned to Europe once more during that locked-out season. Playing for Jokerit in Finland, Thomas continued to post great numbers. In 54 games, Thomas had 34 wins and a save percentage of .946.

When the 2005–2006 season rolled around once more, Thomas returned to Providence to continue playing for the Bruins' minor league team. He played 26 games with a .923 save percentage, good enough to earn him a spot on the Boston Bruins' roster for the second half of the 2005–2006 season.

It also helped that both of Boston's goalies went down with injuries, but Thomas made sure to get the most out of his opportunity. During the summer of 2007, Thomas began a yoga-based physical conditioning program to increase his flexibility and strength, and one that would greatly increase his abilities during the 2007–08 season and onwards

He played 38 games with the big team, notching a .917 save percentage but only 12 wins. The team around him was not very good that year, but with Thomas in the net, they were hoping to turn it around.

After almost nine seasons, Tim Thomas had reached the NHL. This feat is amazing on its own when one considers just how difficult it is to make an NHL roster after several years of not making the cut.

At this point, some would consider Tim Thomas' story a success, but he was not done with his NHL career - not even close!

Thomas continued to play for the Boston Bruins over the next six seasons, and the team reached the playoffs in four of those campaigns. Thomas was selected to four All-Star Games during his time with the Bruins, but the team's biggest success came in the 2010–2011 season. During the regular season, Thomas posted a .938 save percentage, the highest of his NHL career, and a record for any NHL goaltender. He also posted nine shutouts, quite impressive for a goaltender at the NHL level.

The Boston Bruins were good, but they needed Tim Thomas to stop a lot of shots. In the first round of the 2011 playoffs, the Bruins needed seven games to defeat the Montreal Canadiens, and three of those games went to overtime. The Bruins won all three overtime contests.

In the second round, the Bruins decimated the Philadelphia Flyers in four straight games, giving Thomas and his teammates a much-needed rest before the Eastern Conference Finals.

Thomas and the Bruins would need seven games to advance once more, as the Tampa Bay Lightning put up a fight. However, of Boston's four wins, two of them came by way of shutouts by Thomas, including the decisive Game 7 victory. He would also add two more shutouts in the Stanley Cup Finals, helping the Bruins to their first Stanley Cup since 1972. Thomas' shutout in Game 7 was the first time a visiting team had shut out the home team in Game 7 of the Stanley Cup Finals.

For Thomas' efforts, he was rewarded with the Conn Smythe Trophy as the MVP of the 2011 Playoffs. He became only the second American-born player to win the award, and at 37 years old, he is also the oldest to ever win it.

It had been a very long road for Tim Thomas to travel, but he made it to the very top of the NHL with incredible performances when his team needed them the most. He holds the NHL record for most saves in a playoff run with 798. He also has the record for most saves in a Stanley Cup Finals series, with 238.

Tim Thomas played in the NHL for three more seasons, one each with Boston, Florida, and Dallas, though he only played eight games in that final season before stepping back. With two Vezina trophies to his name, Thomas will be remembered as an incredible goaltender who hit his stride in the NHL a bit later than most goalies, but it was all worth the wait. He helped deliver a championship to one of the biggest sports cities in the United States, and he showed that determination and continuously working toward a goal can bring dividends.

## Did You Know?

1. Tim Thomas was born in Flint, Michigan.

2. Thomas was once suspended for failing to report to training camp.

3. Thomas won a silver medal at the 2010 Olympics with Team USA.

4. He was inducted into the Hockey Hall of Fame in 2019.

5. Thomas is the all-time 'wins' leader for the University of Vermont, with 81.

6. Thomas received the Urop Ylonen Award in his first season with the Finnish Elite League.

# CHAPTER 2:

## THE EASTER EPIC

Few NHL games get their own titles, but the ones that do often have incredible stories behind the names. This chapter focuses on one such game that took place on April 18, 1987, between the New York Islanders and the Washington Capitals. It was an incredible event for quite a few reasons, beginning with its importance.

It happened during the 1987 playoffs, first round, also known as the Patrick Division Semifinals. The game took place in Landover, Maryland, where the Capitals played their home games. The Islanders were the third seed in the Eastern Conference, and the Capitals were the second seed.

While the 1980s had been dominated by the Islanders, the Washington Capitals had eliminated the Islanders from the playoffs the year before, so there was a sense that the Islanders wanted to avenge their earliest exit in team history. The series was closely contested throughout, with the Capitals winning Game 1 and the Islanders claiming Game 2. However, the Caps took a commanding lead in the series by winning both games in the Islanders' territory.

Hockey historians quickly pointed out that it had been 12 years since a playoff team had come back to win a series after going down three games to one. The last team to have accomplished that feat, though, was the New York Islanders back in 1975. They also knew they were capable of a comeback against the Capitals team, as just two years before, they became the first team to come back and win a best-of-five series after falling behind 2-0.

The Islanders wanted another chance to do it, and their effort began with a Game 5 win at Washington. Heading back to New York, the Islanders took another step toward history with a Game 6 win. Their two consecutive victories set up the deciding Game 7, with each team at three wins.

The game began at 7:30 p.m., typical of an NHL game. What followed during the contest, however, was anything but typical.

The Capitals were determined to overcome their two previous losses, and they dominated the first period. Mike Gartner found the back of the net behind Islanders' goalie Kelly Hrudey, and the score remained 1-0 for the rest of the frame.

The Islanders did their best to battle back in the second period, getting a goal from Patrick Flatley at the halfway point, but the Capitals were still determined to get the victory. Grant Martin scored for the Capitals before the end of the period, though, restoring Washington's lead with 20 minutes left in the game.

The Hockey Gods can be cruel, though. As time ticked down in the game, both teams playing tough defense and getting great goaltending to shut down any chances, one of the straps on the back of Capitals' goalie Bob Mason's leg

13

pads broke. Because of that broken strap, Mason struggled to squeeze his pads together as a backhand shot from Bryan Trottier came toward the goal.

Mason did his best, but the puck squeezed through his pads and into the back of the net, tying the game with just over five minutes left in the game. With the game all square, the final five minutes of the game were intense as each squad looked for the killing blow. But it did not come, and Game 7 of this epic series was headed to overtime.

While overtime during the regular season is limited, and games often end in a tie, playoff overtime is unlimited. The game continues, with 20-minute overtime periods, until a team scores. When one team scores, the game is immediately over.

As overtime began, both teams found chances to score, but both goaltenders did just enough to keep the puck out. This included a dramatic moment at the end of the first overtime when Greg Smith of Washington took a long-range slapshot that eluded Kelly Hrudey but struck the goal post and ricocheted away from the net.

In the second overtime, it quickly became apparent that the players were getting tired. Instead of quick skating and aggressive play throughout the period, players began looking for ways to slow the game down, to preserve energy until a chance presented itself. The Capitals had 17 shots on goal in that second overtime period, but Hrudey was up to the task. At the other end of the rink, Randy Wood of the Islanders took his turn to hit a goal post, adding more drama to the final periods of the game.

The tension in the arena was immense, as both teams and the sell-out crowd watched in anticipation of victory or defeat. But, with no scoring at the end of the second overtime, the game became the first to reach a third overtime since a matchup between the Rangers and Blackhawks from 16 years prior.

In the third overtime, the Islanders began to get the better of the offensive chances. After being outshot in the second overtime 17-9, New York evened out the possession and shooting chances, but Mason made sure that the puck stayed out of the Capitals' net.

During these overtimes, the clock struck midnight, moving the date from April 18 to April 19, which just happened to be Easter Sunday. The two teams had played long enough for a new day to start, but a victor was yet to emerge.

The Easter Epic continued into a fourth overtime, with both teams exhausted and praying for a victory. It was the first playoff game to reach a fourth overtime since the Canadiens and Red Wings had played it 36 years before this game.

In the seventh period of hockey, both teams were utterly exhausted. As the minutes ticked away, the momentum seemed to be squarely with the Islanders. They were outshooting the Capitals in the fourth overtime when the fateful final play took place. Islander Ken Leiter brought the puck into the offensive zone and slung a pass over to Gord Dineen, who had pinched in to keep the play alive.

Dineen's teammates would later say that they had never seen Dineen so deep in the offensive zone, because Dineen was usually a responsible defensive defenseman. Still, Dineen circled the back of the Capitals' net and then whipped a puck toward the goal. It deflected off a Capitals player and out toward the blue line.

Because Dineen had pinched in deep, New York's star player, Pat LaFontaine, had stayed at the blue line to cover for him. Luckily, Dineen's deflected shot went right to LaFontaine, who caught it on his backhand, spun around, and took an immediate slapshot. The puck found its way through a screen of players in front of the goaltender Mason, who was unable to come up with the save.

The puck bounced off the post, but this time it went into the back of the net, ending the game and the series in an instant. At 1:58 a.m., the New York Islanders had won the hockey game. The shot totals by the end were 75-57 in favor of Washington.

The Islanders came into the next series probably a bit fatigued, as they once again fell behind three games to one to the Philadelphia Flyers. They clawed back to force another Game 7, but they ended up losing Game 7 to end their season.

Though the Islanders could not finish their playoff run in style, the Easter Epic game gave the team the distinction of having won both the longest and shortest series-ending overtime games in NHL history. The longest series-ending overtime game has since been broken when the Dallas Stars defeated the San Jose Sharks in 2008. However, the Islanders still have the longest Game 7 victory in history, which is quite an accomplishment.

The Easter Epic is a prime example of how playoff hockey can create incredible moments in the game. Because of infinite overtime periods that demands a winner be declared, it puts the onus on players to score the winning goal. Multiple overtime periods add to the tension and make that winning goal even more meaningful when it is finally scored.

## Did You Know?

1.  It was the first time in Stanley Cup playoff history that the road team won Game 7 after the first overtime period.

2.  The game ended at the 8:47 mark of the fourth overtime.

3.  It was the only playoff game that season to need multiple overtime periods.

4.  Kelly Hrudey made 73 saves in the game, an NHL record.

5.  The game saw 74 minutes and 10 seconds go by without a goal.

6.  Bobby Gould registered 12 shots on goal without scoring.

# CHAPTER 3:

## MARIO LEMIEUX

Few players in NHL history have made a bigger impact on their team than Mario Lemieux. While other teams across professional sports trade players at will, the Pittsburgh Penguins and Lemieux have stuck together for several decades, and many credit Lemieux for helping the team to the success they have experienced.

Let's examine the incredible career and impact of Mario Lemieux.

Mario was drafted into the Quebec Major Junior Hockey League at the age of 15, and he confidently declared that he would break league records. Turns out, he was right, as he broke the record for most points in a single season. He collected 133 goals and 149 assists in 70 games. After two more seasons in the league, Mario finished with 562 points and had the attention of every team in the NHL. So, when the 1984 draft came around, Lemieux went first overall to the Pittsburgh Penguins, though there was already some tension between the young player and the team.

Early contract negotiations were not going well, so Lemieux did not put on the team's jersey when he was drafted. However, when the team discovered that over 3,000 people had watched Lemieux's selection from the arena, they quickly came to an agreement. For comparison, the team was only drawing about 7,000 people to games, so there was no denying that this young player was already popular among fans of the team.

Little did the organization know, that Mario Lemieux was going to be so much more for the team than a good player. The Penguins had declared bankruptcy nine years earlier, and they were only getting their home arena to half capacity during games. Because of this, the team was in financial trouble. It didn't help that they hadn't made the playoffs for the past few seasons, either. But how could one player change all of that? Well, it might take a long time, but it is possible.

Lemieux didn't wait long to make his mark on the league, as he scored on his very first shift after stealing the puck from future Hall-of-Fame defenseman, Ray Bourque.

From that moment on, Lemieux was a nearly unstoppable force in the league. Later in his first season, he became the first rookie to be named the All-Star Game MVP. By the end of the year, he had 100 points and was awarded the Calder Trophy as the league's best rookie. Even more impressive is that Lemieux missed seven games that season but still reached 100 points.

In his sophomore campaign, Lemieux tallied 141 points, which was only behind Wayne Gretzky's record-breaking campaign of 215 points. Still, Lemieux was voted the best regular-season player by his teammates and opponents.

In his fourth season, he led the Penguins to their first winning record in nine years, though the team finished one point out of the playoff hunt. On an individual level, Lemieux had notched 168 points to win the Art Ross Trophy, awarded to the leading scorer of the league every year. Wayne Gretzky had won the award for the last seven years until Lemieux ended that streak.

Incredibly, Lemieux had not yet reached his peak as a player in the league. In the 1988–89 campaign, Lemieux tallied 199 points, helping the Penguins to their first playoff berth in seven seasons. One highlight of that incredible season was a game against the New Jersey Devils on New Year's Eve when Lemieux scored five goals, one in every possible situation: even strength, power play, penalty kill, penalty shot, and empty net. He is the only player to accomplish this feat.

The Penguins swept the Rangers in the first round of the playoffs that year but fell in a seven-game classic to the Flyers in the second round.

In the following seasons, though, Lemieux began to miss chunks of games due to injuries, including a back injury that evolved into a herniated disc. Though Mario missed 50 regular season games in the 90–91 season due to back surgery, he returned at the end of the season and helped the Penguins win the Stanley Cup, the first in franchise history. He was also awarded the Conn Smythe Trophy as the MVP of the playoffs.

Lemieux missed 18 games in the next season, but he still won the Art Ross Trophy with 131 points before leading the team to another Stanley Cup. Even more impressive, Lemieux suffered a broken hand from a slash in the second round, but it didn't stop him from leading all playoff scorers and winning another Conn Smythe Trophy.

After two Stanley Cups, Lemieux and the Penguins were not slowing down. Mario set a team record by scoring at least once in each of the team's first 12 regular season games. As the season progressed, Lemieux was on pace to challenge the big scoring records set by Wayne Gretzky (92 goals in one season and 215 points in one season). However, in January 1993, Lemieux was diagnosed with Hodgkin Lymphoma, a type of cancer affecting the lymphatic system.

Lemieux had to miss time, seemingly indefinitely, to receive treatment. Fans and players alike mourned Mario's health situation, wishing him the best, but no one quite knew what would happen.

Two months later, Mario Lemieux unexpectedly returned to the lineup on the very day of his last radiation treatment. Incredibly, the crowd in Philadelphia gave him a standing ovation, even though he played for their team's rival.

When he returned to the lineup, Lemieux was 12 points behind Pat LaFontaine for the NHL scoring lead, and he finished the season with another scoring title, 12 points ahead of LaFontaine, even though he played 24 fewer games in the process.

Lemieux wouldn't win another Stanley Cup as a player for the team, but he did become the team's owner in 1999 when financial troubles emerged again. As the owner of the organization, he helped stabilize the team's finances, including after his retirement from the league during the 2005–06 season.

Unfortunately, part of that stabilization came at the cost of the Penguins' roster. The team missed the playoffs beginning in 2002 until 2006, but it also gave the team the opportunity to draft Sidney Crosby, who would become the face of the franchise for the next decade and beyond.

In fact, with Lemieux as part-owner of the team, Pittsburgh would find more success as soon as 2009, winning a Stanley Cup with Crosby as the captain. To ensure that no one thought it was a fluke, the Penguins won back-to-back championships in 2016 and 2017 as well, adding to Mario's legacy as the single most important person to the franchise.

Mario Lemieux's career, both on the ice and in the front office, propelled the Pittsburgh Penguins to the top of the NHL on multiple occasions. He helped the team avoid moving away from the city of Pittsburgh and ensured the financial stability of the franchise in the long term.

On the ice, Mario Lemieux was a force. He was elected to the Hockey Hall of Fame back in 1997, just after his first attempt at retirement. He has won five Stanley Cups, two as a player, and three as an owner. He has six Art Ross Trophies, four Ted Lindsay Awards, and three Hart Memorial Trophies. He was selected to 12 All-Star games and had four All-Star MVP performances.

Internationally, competing for Team Canada, Lemieux collected three gold medals, one each in the Canada Cup in 1987, the Winter Olympics in 2002, and the World Cup of Hockey in 2004. For his international efforts, Lemieux was elected to the International Ice Hockey Federation Hall of Fame in 2008.

Mario Lemieux's career is the purest definition of an incredible hockey story. He played the game at the highest level for his entire life, and he couldn't even be stopped by a cancer diagnosis. And then, when his team needed help to stay in the city of Pittsburgh, Mario Lemieux leveraged his deferred salary into equity for ownership of the team.

At every turn, Mario Lemieux gave everything he had to the game he loved. He is a true ambassador of the game and an incredible person.

## Did You Know?

1. Lemieux is the only person to have his name on the Stanley Cup as a player and an owner.

2. He won the Lester B. Pearson Award four times as the MVP voted by players.

3. Because of injuries, Mario Lemieux never played a complete regular season schedule.

4. In his later years, the back pain was so bad that he needed help tying his skates.

5. Lemieux became the third player ever to continue playing after being inducted into the Hall of Fame.

6. In the city of Pittsburgh, there is a statue of his likeness that was erected in March 2012.

# CHAPTER 4:

## ANGELA JAMES

The modern game of hockey, and most sports in general, favors male athletes, leaving very little room for women to make themselves known as skilled and talented players. Therefore, when a woman does make a mark on the sport, you can be sure that she is an incredible person who deserves a chapter in this book.

Angela James is one such incredible hockey player.

James grew up in a mixed-race family, and she was bullied in school because of how different she looked from her mother. This treatment caused James to grow up in a combative environment, fighting to protect herself and her family. She carried that mentality to the ice rink, making her a force to be reckoned with when playing hockey.

Angela played many sports as a child, and though her mother wanted her to focus on swimming, Angela selected hockey. One can understand why her mother did not want her daughter to focus on hockey in the 1970s, as there were few opportunities for women players at that time.

However, Angela pressed forward, beginning by dominating her neighborhood league, even after she was moved from the novice league to the peewee league. She was eight years old but competing against 11 and 12-year-olds. She only competed in this league for one year before the league banned girls from playing. Rumor was that the president's son was on her team, and he didn't like that Angela was getting the praise.

Forced to find another place to play, Angela's mother had to take her by bus to Annunciation, a Catholic organization in another district. A few years later, at age 13, Angela had to play against girls and women 16 and older when she played for the Newtonbrook Saints at the Senior C level, which was the fourth-highest level of women's hockey in Toronto.

Because Angela focused so much on hockey, her schoolwork often was lacking. She needed help graduating high school, and her situation at Seneca College was not much better. After several arguments with her hockey coach, she began to put more effort into her education.

On the ice, her coach also challenged her by changing the position she played. Instead of being a forward, she was asked to play defense. Up to the challenge, James still led the league in scoring. In her second season the team, James scored 30 points in 10 games, leading the team to its first-ever championship. She was also voted the MVP of the league.

James and Seneca College followed up this performance with another championship. James dominated the league almost by herself, scoring 50 goals in 14 games. One local newspaper called her the Wayne Gretzky of women's hockey.

In conjunction with her college competitions, James was also playing Senior level hockey all around Ontario. She played for the Toronto Islanders of the Central Ontario Women's Hockey League beginning in 1980, and she quickly made a name for herself at the Senior AA level, the highest level of women's hockey at the time. The first women's national championship, which took place in 1982, featured a game-tying goal and victory for James over Team Alberta.

James was becoming well known for her dominating performances, and her style of hockey was spoken of around the country. Her skating strength allowed her to play a physical game, using strong positioning to win puck battles along the boards. Hockey historians maintain that James helped break the stereotype that women wouldn't, or couldn't, play a gritty style of hockey.

Some compared her to the pure goal scorers of the NHL, like Mike Bossy or Mark Messier.

Over the next 17 years of hockey, Angela James would feature in 12 national championship tournaments, even though she frequently moved from one team to another.

Internationally, Angela James represented Team Canada at several events. In 1990, she competed in the World Championships, where her team won gold. She was also on the roster for gold medals in Finland in 1992, Lake Placid in 1994, and Kitchener in 1997.

She even competed in the first women's world championship back in 1987, though it was not sponsored by the International Ice Hockey Federation. James' Team Ontario reached the finals of that tournament, ultimately losing to Team Canada, whom she could have played with. However, she had been selected to represent her home team, and the team performed quite well against opponents from all around the world.

However, there was a controversial event that took place during the run-up to what would be the first Olympic tournament for women's hockey. At the 1998 Nagano Games, Team Canada's head coach, Shannon Miller, did not include Angela on the roster for the tournament, even though she had been the team's leading goal scorer in the preliminary games leading up to the tournament.

Rumors swirled around the decision, as some unknown individuals even insinuated that the coach was sleeping with a member of the team. There was no evidence of any foul play, though, but James was not on the roster due to this misinformation. Team Canada would go on to lose in the Gold Medal Match to the United States.

Some of James' teammates argued after the tournament ended that had James been included, the outcome of the tournament would have been better for their team.

Outside of her playing career, James has also been involved in the refereeing and coaching side of the game. As a coach, she led her former team, Seneca College, to an Ontario College Championship in 1987. She was also an assistant coach at the 1999 Canada Winter Games, where her team won a gold medal.

As a referee, she has been an active official since 1980. She has gained level IV certification with Hockey Canada, even serving as the Ontario Women's Hockey Association's Referee-in-Chief.

Today, James is part-owner and General Manager of the Toronto Six, a team in the Premier Hockey Federation.

Thankfully, Angela James has been well recognized and awarded for her hockey accomplishments over the years. Many consider her to be the "first superstar of modern women's hockey," and her efforts have been credited for pioneering and growing the game on an international scale.

It's not that women's players before James were not skilled. It's that her strong style of play legitimized and brought credibility to the game itself. Before James, many would judge the women's game as too soft, or not real hockey. Angela James changed all of that, and because she did, the women's game earned respect around the world. Some even assert that women's hockey would not have become an Olympic event without James' contributions to the sport.

At the senior level, James was an eight-time scoring leader and was also voted the MVP six times. In 2005, Hockey Canada honored her with the Female Hockey Breakthrough Award. The arena in Flemington Park, where James first played organized hockey, was renamed in her honor.

The Canadian Women's Hockey League awards the Angela James Bowl to the scoring leader each season. James was also one of the first women inducted into both the IIHF and Hockey Halls of Fame.

Angela James was a trailblazer for women's hockey. Through her tenacity and skill, she demonstrated that an incredible hockey player could be of any gender. She could play a brand of hockey like those played by men, and she could excel with her unique skillset.

## Did You Know?

1. In 2021, James was named to the Order of Hockey in Canada.

2. James is the only African Canadian to serve as captain of a national hockey team.

3. She was inducted into the Hockey Hall of Fame along with Cammi Granato.

4. James held the OCAA record for goals and points until the league disbanded.

5. She was also inducted into the Seneca Valley Hall of Fame, and her jersey number was retired there.

6. In the NWHL, she was named MVP six times.

# CHAPTER 5:

## MESSIER DELIVERS FOR THE RANGERS

Mark Messier is a household name for most NHL fans these days, as he experienced a lot of success on the ice in the 1980s. But when he was moved to the New York Rangers, a team that had not won a Stanley Cup in decades, many wondered if he would be able to deliver the same success. The story that followed demonstrated that Mark Messier was one of the true leaders in the history of the game.

Let's examine the story of Mark Messier.

As a teenager, Mark's father was part of the coaching staff of the junior Spruce Grove Mets, a team of the Alberta Junior Hockey League, so Mark decided to try out at the age of 15. While the age limit of the league was 20 years old, Mark surprisingly made the team, where he went on to collect 66 points in 57 games.

A year later, the team relocated and became the St. Albert Saints, and then they named Mark Messier their captain. To reward the team for the honor, Mark scored 74 points in 54 games. After the end of the season, he played seven games for the Portland Winterhawks of the junior Western Hockey League, scoring five points in seven playoff games.

Feeling like he had out grown the Alberta league, Mark began seeking an alternative. As it turns out, the Indianapolis Racers of the World Hockey Association were looking for a talented player to replace another player they had just traded, Wayne Gretzky.

Messier played five games with the Racers but refused to sign a contract for longer, which was a good decision, as the team folded, and his first check bounced.

After a few months with the Cincinnati Stingers, the WHA folded at the end of the season, leaving Mark with few options but to enter the 1979 NHL Entry Draft. He was selected by the Edmonton Oilers in the third round, and his first year caused issues.

He seemed to struggle with the rigid schedule of the professional league, as he was disciplined by the team for missing a team flight. However, the team noticed that he was a strong leader in the locker room and that developed further as he acclimated to the league.

He improved his scoring as the years progressed, and in the 1984 playoffs, he moved from wing to center, helping the Oilers win their first Stanley Cup. He earned the Conn Smythe Trophy as the playoff MVP for his strong performance.

Despite finding lots of success with the Oilers, including four more Stanley Cups, Messier still had occasional issues that took away from his game. In 1984, Messier received a ten-game suspension after he sucker punched Jamie Macoun of the Calgary Flames. Macoun had boarded Messier earlier in the game, but the league ruled that Messier had instigated the fight with the sucker punch. Macoun's cheekbone was broken in the attack.

The next year, in 1985, Messier was charged with a hit and run after striking three parked cars with his Porsche. He was able to pay a fine and avoid jail time for the incident.

This trouble was in sharp contrast with his performances on the ice, as he was a focal point of the Oilers' offense during those five Stanley Cup championships. Still, Messier was considered a good leader for the team, but his happiness with the organization dissolved one year after their last championship, in the summer of 1991.

Adam Graves, a teammate and friend of Messier, left the Oilers team that summer and Messier was upset that the organization was not willing to pay to keep Graves on the roster. As it turned out, the team was looking to save money, so they also decided to trade Messier. They sent him to the New York Rangers in exchange for three players.

The Rangers of the time were a good team, but they were unable to make deep runs into the playoffs. The team acquired Messier in the hopes that his leadership would be the missing key to help them end their Stanley Cup drought. He wasn't just skilled, the team thought. They hoped that he could teach them how to win it all.

Which would prevail? Analysts wondered if Messier's winning ways would be contagious, or if the championship drought would continue to haunt the Rangers.

In his first home game with the team, the Rangers named Messier their captain, and their journey together was underway.

Early in his tenure, he began to take control of the culture in the locker room when he found a player's jersey left on the floor after a game. He picked up the jersey and called the attention of his teammates. He told them that the crest on the jersey needed to be respected, because of the many great NHL players who had worn it in the past.

He wanted to establish pride in the concept of the team, and his efforts were paying off. In his first season with the team, Messier won his second Hart Trophy as the league MVP, and the team won the Presidents' Trophy for the best record in the league. However, that great season came to a halt when the eventual champion Pittsburgh Penguins defeated the Rangers in the second round of the playoffs.

There was disappointment in New York, but that disappointment would be amplified during the 1992–93 season when the Rangers finished last in their division and missed the playoffs. It was the first time in Mark Messier's NHL career that he was not participating in the playoffs. Messier was even famously booed by the crowd in Madison Square Garden, where the Rangers play their home games.

At the end of the season, many wondered if Messier was a bust, while others speculated that Messier would leave the team to their losing ways. Instead, Messier and the Rangers decided to refocus and get back to business. The team changed coaches, so there was a new energy in the locker room and on the ice.

The Rangers recovered from their failures of the previous season, and they returned to the top of their division, once again winning the Presidents' Trophy for the league's best record.

This time, the fans had an even stronger hope that their quest for the Stanley Cup would be completed successfully. After a quick sweep of the New York Islanders in the first round, followed by a 4-1 series win over the Washington Capitals, the Rangers faced off against the New Jersey Devils in the Eastern Conference Finals.

The first game of the series was the kind that often breaks a team's spirit. The Rangers were ahead late in the third period, 3-2 when Claude Lemieux scored a goal to tie the game and send it to overtime. Though the Rangers fought hard, they fell in double overtime to a goal by Stephane Richer. They bounced back in Game 2 with a shutout, then they found a way to win a double overtime game on the road in Game 3, taking a 2-1 series lead.

However, the Devils responded with two straight wins in Games 4 and 5, putting the Rangers at risk of elimination going into Game 6. The Rangers practiced in New Jersey the day before the game, and after practice, Messier sat down to speak with a huge group of reporters. One of them asked Mark what he thought would happen in Game 6.

Most players would have a political answer about how they would go out and play their game, execute the plan, and focus on what they needed to do. Mark Messier wanted to send a message to his teammates, though, when they opened the newspaper on the day of the game.

"We know we have to win it. We can win it and we are going to win it," he said.

He admitted later that he didn't think about the Devils players and fans reading the same newspaper, but his comments caught the attention of the hockey world. All eyes were on Mark Messier and the Rangers, eager to see if he would be successful or have to eat his words.

At the end of the first period, the Devils are ahead 2-0 with their home ice crowd excited to advance to the Stanley Cup Finals.

As the second period progressed, though, Messier was determined to lead his team to victory. He carried the puck into the offensive zone, then dropped a pass to Alexei Kovalev, who fired a shot past Martin Brodeur to cut the lead in half, 2-1. With one assist heading into the third period, Messier knew there was more work to be done.

What followed was one of the best individual performances in NHL history. Mark Messier scored two goals on Brodeur, then added the empty-net dagger as his hat trick goal, giving the Rangers a 4-2 victory, and a chance to win the series in the upcoming Game 7.

And, of course, Game 7 went to double overtime, and of course, the Rangers were victorious. All that remained between the Rangers and glory were the Vancouver Canucks.

After another grueling seven-game series, the Rangers were victorious, winning the Stanley Cup and proving that the Rangers had selected the right man to be their captain.

Mark Messier led his team on an incredible playoff run, winning some of the best playoff series ever played.

## Did You Know?

1. Out of any professional athlete active in the 1970s, Messier was the last to retire.

2. His nickname was "The Moose".

3. In his playing career, he won six Stanley Cups.

4. A leadership award was named after Messier, and it is presented annually to the NHL player who shows great leadership qualities on and off the ice.

5. Messier's number was retired by the Rangers in 2006.

6. On the all-time points list, Messier is third behind only Wayne Gretzky and Gordie Howe.

# CHAPTER 6:

## WILLIE O'REE

Ice hockey's biggest league is the National Hockey League, which operates in the United States and Canada. The U.S., unfortunately, has a dark history when it comes to slavery and lingering racism. Because of that history, it was a big moment in each of the professional sports leagues when a Black player was able to make it onto a roster for the first time. Even though the United States had fought a Civil War and ended slavery, opportunities were still kept away from Black individuals for no good reason.

However, when a special person comes along who is both skilled enough to make the roster and brave enough to face the racism of others throughout an entire country, they change the course of sports history. Willie O'Ree is that player for ice hockey. Let's take a look at the incredible life and career of the first Black NHL player.

Way back in 1935, Willie O'Ree was born in New Brunswick, Canada, where he grew up playing hockey. As he worked his way through the youth leagues, he gained momentum as his game progressed, eventually making it on the roster of the Quebec Aces, a minor league team.

While this was impressive on its own, O'Ree had also suffered a significant injury during his time on the team when a puck struck him in the face. The doctors on the team made sure that Willie was not seriously injured, and he convinced them that nothing was wrong. However,

O'Ree concealed the fact that he no longer had any vision in his right eye. Not only was Willie O'Ree playing hockey at a high level, but he was also now doing it with only one working eye!

O'Ree maintained this secret for several years because he knew that he would not be allowed into the NHL if they ever found out about the injury.

During his second season with the Quebec Aces, only one eye functional, Willie was called up to the NHL ranks by the Boston Bruins. They needed a replacement player to cover for one of their starters who had to miss time because of an illness. It was temporary, his call-up, but it was enough to make Willie O'Ree the first Black player to compete in the NHL, and it took place on January 18, 1958, in a game against the Montreal Canadiens. O'Ree would get the call-up one more time that season, but then it would be two more years with the Quebec Aces before Boston came calling once more.

This time, though, O'Ree would stick around for a whole lot longer. In the 1960–61 regular season, O'Ree played 43 games with the Boston Bruins, which was more than half of the 70-game season schedule. However, with so many games at the highest level, and given the era, there were bound to be incidents caused by individuals who were not prepared to play against a Black player or watch a Black player play the sport.

One particularly nasty incident took place in Chicago when the Bruins faced off against the Blackhawks. As it often happens, though, a terrible incident can lead to positive changes.

A Blackhawks player by the name of Eric Nesterenko hit O'Ree in the face with the butt-end of his stick, which is a severe penalty in hockey no matter where a player is struck. It was a disgusting play that knocked out O'Ree's two front teeth and broke his nose. It was quite clear that the attack was out of line and didn't have a place in the game of hockey. However, since it had happened, Willie O'Ree had to respond. And he did.

At this point, since Nesterenko had abandoned all sense of sportsmanship and gentlemanly play, O'Ree did the same. He took his stick and struck Nesterenko over the head with it. A play like that in today's game would likely get a player permanently expelled from the league, but today's NHL is vastly different from its predecessor. Instead, both players continued to play in that very same contest. No ejections, no suspensions.

This did not sit well with the Blackhawks players and fans. For the rest of the game, people hurled racial slurs at O'Ree and became incensed when he played the puck. It didn't help that O'Ree's retaliation against Nesterenko would have been easily visible from anywhere in the arena, while Nesterenko's butt-end attack could have gone mostly unnoticed. Regardless, it was a dangerous situation.

Later, O'Ree would say that he thought it was only luck that got him out of that arena with his life. I don't know about you, but if that had happened to me, and 20,000 people were seemingly out for my blood, I'm not sure I would have the courage to keep playing the game I love. O'Ree, though, was undeterred.

After that season, Willie O'Ree did not make another appearance in the NHL, but he moved on and found success with the Los Angeles Blades and San Diego Gulls of the Western Hockey League. Statistically, O'Ree averaged more than one point per game, and he also won two scoring titles.

Willie O'Ree continued to play competitively for several years, only hanging up the skates at 43 years old. And while many NHL players have come and gone, few have made such a positive impact on the league and the game as Willie O'Ree.

If you're wondering what kind of impact O'Ree made on the sport, outside of being the first player to break the color barrier, you might be surprised to learn that Willie didn't retire to a life of peace and solitude. Instead, Willie spent his retirement working as an ambassador for the game.

He wanted to make a difference for the young people interested in the game, no matter the color of their skin. The NHL also took action based on O'Ree's experiences and now includes diversity training during every NHL preseason for players and coaches. The league also implemented rules that effectively outlaw the use of racist language and verbal abuse, making any offenses punishable by fines and suspensions.

O'Ree also received recognition from organizations all over the continent, including the New Brunswick Hall of Fame, where he was inducted in 1984. He was also named the Diversity Ambassador for the NHL, and he was paid to travel around the continent and promote the sport at schools and community centers. On his travels, he would spread ideas of inclusion, dedication, and confidence, and show how those ideals could serve a young person both on and off the ice.

Willie also worked with the NHL to develop the NHL/USA Hockey Diversity Task Force, and after its founding, he served as the director of youth development.

More recently, Willie O'Ree was honored by the Boston Bruins in 2008 to celebrate the 50th anniversary of his first time competing in the NHL. As part of that celebration, there was a special exhibit on display at the Sports Museum of New England. The Canadian government also bestowed him with the Order of Canada, a title that represents honor for Canadian civilians.

Overall, Willie O'Ree may not have had an incredible NHL career, but his impact on the sport of ice hockey cannot be overstated. He paved the way for young players of color who once believed they would not be welcomed by the sport and its community.

In today's NHL, the majority of players are White, but there are several players of color who have made significant impacts on the game. One of those players, Joel Ward, mentioned O'Ree by name as one of the people who inspired Joel to pursue the game of hockey.

Willie O'Ree's dedication to spreading the game of hockey, along with qualities that build a strong character, helped grow the sport more than most players who made it to the league. His impact is something that will continue to grow as racism is slowly eradicated from sports and society, and that is pretty incredible.

## Did You Know?

1. Willie was the youngest of 13 siblings.

2. When the weather permitted, Willie would skate to school.

3. His older brother taught him how to throw a bodycheck.

4. At 14, Willie met baseball legend Jackie Robinson, another player to break a sport's color barrier.

5. Art Dorrington was the first Black player to sign with a pro team, but he never played.

6. O'Ree was inducted into the Hockey Hall of Fame as a builder of the sport.

# CHAPTER 7:

## THE ISLANDERS' DYNASTY

There are great NHL teams throughout the history of the league, but few have as many accolades as the New York Islanders of the early 1980s. Let's examine how this team was a cut above the rest for several years, and how their accomplishments put them at the top of all-time teams in the history of the sport.

After the team's founding in 1972, along with the Atlanta Flames, there were a total of 16 teams in the NHL, but the Islanders were not ready to compete with the best teams. Their youth and inexperience at the highest level of hockey were apparent, as the team only won 12 out of 80 regular season games in that first year. At the time, it was the NHL record for the most losses and worst overall record in a single season.

With that last-place finish, though, the Islanders were to select first for the 1973 draft, and they selected Denis Potvin, a highly desired defenseman. The team was making improvements, and although they finished last in their division once more, their defense had improved significantly, as they allowed 100 fewer goals 'against' when compared to that first dreadful season.

The 1974 draft was another key building block for the Islanders, as they had the 4th and 22nd picks in the first round, which they used to select Clark Gillies and Bryan Trottier. With those picks combined with the core of players quickly learning the NHL game, the team made a big jump, earning 32 more points in the standings than the previous season. It was enough to send the Islanders on their first trip to the playoffs.

However, the future dynasty was not yet ready. The team was showing promise, though, as they defeated the Rangers in the best-of-three first round, then overcame a 3-0 deficit in the second round to beat the Penguins in a seven-game thriller. They even came back from another 3-0 deficit before losing to the eventual champion Philadelphia Flyers in Game 7 of the Eastern Conference Finals.

It was a good start, and the team showed tenacity, but pieces were missing.

In the 1975–76 season, they finished with 101 points in the standings, fifth-best in the league, but lost to Montreal in the playoffs. Still, they struck gold once more in the 1977 draft when they selected Mike Bossy, and by the end of the season, he had won the Calder Trophy, the third Islander to win it. This is impressive when one remembers it was only their fifth season in the league.

As the team continued to improve, they still found difficulty making it deep into the playoffs, as they lost to the Canadiens once more in 1978. Things were especially tense around the organization when the Islanders went into the 1979 playoffs with the best regular season record but crashed out of the playoffs when they were upset by their rivals, the New York Rangers.

But legendary coach Al Arbour had a solution going into the following season. Instead of focusing on the grind of the regular season, the team would conserve energy and prepare for the playoffs. For the first time in five years, the Islanders finished the 1979–80 season with fewer than 100 points, but they were ready for the playoffs. In fact, they were ready for every playoff season for quite a while.

It also helped that the team traded for second-line center Butch Goring, who many historians of the game consider as being the "final piece of the puzzle."

The Islanders would go on to defeat Los Angeles, Boston, Buffalo, and the Philadelphia Flyers to win their first Stanley Cup championship.

That series with Philadelphia was considered one of the best series ever played, as Philadelphia had entered the playoffs on a legendary hot streak. They had gone undefeated for 35 straight games to end the regular season, but that momentum ran out at the last possible moment. The Islanders won the series in six games, and the final overtime goal was the moment that Islanders fans had been waiting for.

What happened next, and what continued to happen, no one could have expected. After all, it was wild enough to consider that the Islanders didn't exist when the 1971–72 season was played, but now they were raising the Stanley Cup at the end of the 1980 playoffs. Surely it was a nice sentiment, but they couldn't do it again, right?

Well, it turns out they could. And, to make sure everyone knew what was coming, the Islanders decided they were good enough to perform well in the regular season *and* the playoffs. At the end of the 1980–81 season, the Islanders were at the top of their division with 110 points, 13 points ahead of the second-place team, Philadelphia.

The 1981 playoffs were not much different, as the Islanders swept the Maple Leafs, beat Wayne Gretzky, Mark Messier, and the Edmonton Oilers in six games, swept the Rangers, and then beat the Minnesota North Stars in five games to win another cup. Butch Goring, the "final piece of the puzzle," won the Conn Smythe Trophy as the playoff MVP.

The team was unstoppable!

During the next season, they won 15 straight games (a record at the time) as they set a franchise record for points on the season with 118. Mike Bossy had 147 points in 80 games, a record for the right-wing position.

When the playoffs rolled around, though, they were trailing the Pittsburgh Penguins in the deciding Game 5 but were able to tie the game and win the series in overtime. It was their ninth straight playoff series victory, but they weren't done yet. They moved on to defeat the Rangers in six games, then they swept two Canadian teams, the Quebec Nordiques and the Vancouver Canucks, to win their third Stanley Cup in a row. This time, Bossy was awarded the Conn Smythe.

With three cups under their belts, many around the league began to wonder if Wayne Gretzky and the Oilers were ready for their turn to win. As it turns out, the two teams were fated to meet and settle the debate on the ice.

The Islanders finished with 96 points, 10 points back of the Flyers, but still made the playoffs. They defeated the Capitals in four games before meeting the Rangers once again in the second round. Another six-game series and the Islanders advanced once more, where they faced the Bruins. Still, the Islanders prevailed, and they were headed to their fourth Stanley Cup Finals.

On the other side of the bracket, after sweeping Winnipeg, beating Calgary four games to one, and then sweeping Chicago, Wayne Gretzky and the Edmonton Oilers were ready for their chance to win it all.

It was the series that the hockey world had been waiting for. The league MVP Wayne Gretzky was looking to dethrone the three-time champions.

What followed was anything but exciting. After the Islanders won both games in Edmonton to take a 2-0 lead heading back to Long Island, many thought Gretzky and company could claw their way back. However, New York continued to pour it on, winning Game 3 by a decisive four-goal margin before taking Game 4 and the Stanley Cup with a 4-2 victory.

Billy Smith, the Islanders' goaltender, took the MVP honors this playoff season, and for good reason, as he and the Islander defense had found a way to stop the high-scoring Gretzky long enough to win their fourth straight championship.

Gretzky, for his part, recalled that he had walked by the Islanders locker room after the final game of the series, expecting to hear partying and cheering. Instead, he saw the Islanders covered in ice packs and taking care of their bodies. It gave Gretzky the incentive to take the game more seriously, and that message would sink in for him and his team in the following years.

The Islanders would reach the Stanley Cup Finals again in 1984, but they would lose to those same Oilers in five games. New York had won 19 straight playoff series, won four straight Stanley Cups, and dominated an entire professional sports league for nearly half a decade. It was a legendary, incredible run that will likely never be matched again.

Sure, the Canadiens had their runs back during the Original Six days, but they simply had fewer opponents. Yes, the Stanley Cup has always been the most difficult trophy to win, but it was simply easier to do back then. The Islanders played in an ever-growing league with more talent showing up every day, and they still got the job done for nearly five full years.

It was, truly, an incredible dynasty.

## Did You Know?

1. The team was bought by a new owner the season before all the winnings began.

2. Most of the contributing players on the team were drafted by the organization.

3. During the 81-82 season, the Islanders won 15 games in a row.

4. Duane and Brent Sutter scored 12 combined points in the first three games of the 83 Finals.

5. Mike Bossy scored 50 goals in 50 games during the 1981 campaign.

6. The 19 straight playoff series victories comprised the longest streak in all of professional sports.

# CHAPTER 8:

## THE COLORADO AVALANCHE AND DETROIT RED WINGS RIVALRY

In the world of professional sports, rivalries sometimes develop when two teams have to compete against each other a bit more often than usual. It also helps if both of those teams are competitive, and if the games being played between them are meaningful to the outcome of their respective campaigns. Every once in a while, though, two teams in this position will add dynamite to the mix, making it a captivating battle between two sets of players over years and years of games. In this case, the catalyst was one player's broken face.

The Colorado Avalanche and Detroit Red Wings were two teams in the NHL's Western Conference that were both ascending the standings around the same period in hockey history.

For Detroit's part, Steve Yzerman had been on the roster for over a decade, dragging the team along as they slowly improved and began making the playoffs in the early 1990s.

Colorado, meanwhile, was newly formed in 1995 after the team left the city of Quebec behind and started anew in Denver, Colorado. Much of the roster followed, and they added pieces such as Patrick Roy and Claude Lemieux to accelerate their success in a new city.

The teams battled during the 1995–1996 regular season, but it wasn't until the 1996 Western Conference Finals that things boiled over. The Avs won Games 1 and 2 in Detroit to take a commanding lead in the series, so the Wings were desperate to fight back. During Game 3, Slava Kozlov of Detroit dodged a check from Colorado defenseman Adam Foote, then slammed Foote's head into the glass with his hand, leaving Foote bleeding from his forehead.

In retaliation, later in the game, as the two teams were arguing and pushing after a whistle, Lemieux found Kozlov on the ice and sucker punched him in the face, which earned him a suspension for Game 4. The Wings won Game 3, lost Game 4, and then won Game 5. The series was 3-2 in favor of Colorado, who had another chance to win the series, but this time they were on home ice.

With just under six minutes left in the first period of Game 6, Lemieux checked Red Wing Kris Draper from behind, driving Draper's face into the top part of the boards, called a dasher, right in front of the Red Wings bench. Draper collapsed to the ice, holding his face as blood dripped from it in a steady flow.

Draper was taken to a hospital and treated for a broken jaw, along with shattered cheek and orbital bones. The Avalanche would go on to win Game 6, sending them to the Stanley Cup Finals, where they swept the Florida Panthers and claimed their first Cup in their first year as the Colorado Avalanche.

During the next season, the teams played each other four times. Lemieux did not play in the first two of those matchups because of an abdominal injury that sidelined him. During the third game, the Colorado coaching staff tried to keep Lemieux off the ice whenever Detroit's enforcer, Darren McCarty, was skating.

On March 26, 1997, in Detroit's Joe Louis Arena, the two teams met for the fourth time that season. The game would come to be known as Fight Night at the Joe, as multiple fights took place during the contest.

At the end of the first period, after two fights had already taken place, the tension boiled over. As Peter Forsberg of the Avalanche and Igor Larionov of the Red Wings became tangled and wrestled each other to the ice, McCarty escaped the grips of Adam Foote to attack Lemieux, who went down to the ice and curled up to protect himself from McCarty's attack. Avalanche goaltender Patrick Roy joined the fray at center ice, leaping at Red Wings forward Brendan Shanahan before the Red Wings goaltender, Mike Vernon, could trade punches with Roy.

McCarty dragged Lemieux over near the Red Wings bench and continued striking him, even trying to knee Lemieux in the face. When Lemieux and McCarty were separated, there was a small puddle of blood on the ice where Lemieux's face had been bleeding.

Standing on the Red Wings bench, looking down at the red stain on the white ice, was Kris Draper, who had been injured by Lemieux a year before. The fighting continued in the second period, and by the end of the game, there had been 18 fighting penalties assessed and a total of 144 penalty minutes on the scoresheet. Once the fighting died down, the Red Wings won that fourth game in overtime.

The two teams met in the Western Conference Finals once again that year, but this time it was Detroit winning the series in six games. They went on to win their first Stanley Cup in 42 years by sweeping the Philadelphia Flyers.

The next season, the two teams did not meet in the playoffs, but during a game on April 1, they played each other again, and more fights took place. Patrick Roy and Chris Osgood, the teams' goaltenders, met at center ice to fight, basically mirroring the events of the year before. The Red Wings went on to win their second straight Cup, but Colorado was ready to win some of their own once again.

In 1999, they met in the second round of the playoffs, and the Avalanche won the series in six games after falling behind 2-0. Colorado would not make it to the Finals, but they had defeated Detroit, at least.

In 2000, it was more of the same, as the two strong teams met in the second round. Once again, Colorado was victorious, this time only needing five games to eliminate their rivals. Colorado didn't win the Cup, but they seemed the closer of the two teams at the time to achieve that feat.

Sure enough, in 2001, the Avalanche would capture their second Stanley Cup, without having to beat Detroit on their way there.

In 2002, there was one final episode between these two teams, and of course, it featured Avalanche goaltender Patrick Roy. On March 23, as the teams were playing in Denver, Red Wings forward Kirk Maltby crashed into the Colorado net, angering Roy, who began throwing punches at Maltby as players around the net began grabbing each other to fight.

The Red Wings goaltender that year was Dominik Hasek, who was not known for his physicality. Even still, Hasek made his way down the ice, removing his glove and blocker as he did, prepared to fight. Roy did not see him coming, though, and when Hasek got close, he tripped on a loose stick on the ice and slid into the back of Roy's legs, tripping him and bringing the referees over to keep them separated.

While it was not the fireworks that everyone wanted to see, it was the end of a fierce rivalry that had lasted for nearly seven years, all spawning from one terrible check. There were three generations of goaltender fights, as Patrick Roy was prepared to do battle with whoever was wearing the pads and the winged wheel at the other end of the rink.

Kris Draper would continue helping the Red Wings. They won the Stanley Cup in 2002 to put an exclamation point on the rivalry, as they had to defeat the Avalanche to reach the Finals. Most notably, the series went seven games, but instead of a close game, the Red Wings won the deciding game by a 7-0 margin. Patrick Roy was pulled from the game, and after that season, the rivalry fizzled.

Today, the two teams are in different divisions, so they do not play each other as often. As it happens, the Red Wings are in a slump, having missed the playoffs for several seasons in a row, while Colorado won another Stanley Cup in 2022. Perhaps if both teams simultaneously rise once more and meet in the Stanley Cup Finals one day, there might just be a spark leftover from the bloody battles that took place over two decades ago.

## Did You Know?

1. The Detroit News printed a "wanted" poster with a picture of Claude Lemieux before the big fight in 1997.

2. Colorado coach Marc Crawford screamed at Wings coach Scotty Bowman during Game 4 of the 1997 playoff matchup, and he was fined $10,000 for his actions.

3. The two teams are tied in their playoff head-to-head matchup, as they have both won 17 games.

4. The two teams met in the 2016 NHL Stadium Series, where the Red Wings prevailed.

5. Former Red Wing Darren Helm won a Stanley Cup with the Avalanche in 2022.

6. Cale Makar won the Norris and Conn Smythe in the same season, just as Nicklas Lidstrom did with the Red Wings in 2002.

# CHAPTER 9:

## JAGR SPARKS A COMEBACK

The scene is the 1992 Stanley Cup Finals. The Chicago Blackhawks and the Pittsburgh Penguins are meeting to decide which team will get to lift that legendary trophy at the end of a best-of-seven series. Mario Lemieux and his team are facing off against Ed Belfour and Chris Chelios of Chicago in what many expected to be a tough series for both squads.

This incredible story, though, only focuses on one game of that series, and it is the first one. Many analysts and hockey stat geeks will tell you that winning the first game of a playoff series greatly increases your chances of winning the series outright. In fact, teams that win the first game will go on to win the series 68% of the time, which is not an amazing odd, but they are pretty good.

So, let's take a look at Game 1 of the 1992 Stanley Cup Finals to see which of these two teams came out on top, and all of the drama that unfolded to reach that result.

The game took place on Pittsburgh's home ice, as they finished with a better record during the regular season. However, the Blackhawks were not going to let the home crowd into the game. Early in the first period, the Blackhawks found themselves with a power play opportunity after some good forechecking in the Penguins' zone. The faceoff was won back to the Blackhawks defenseman Chris Chelios, who sidestepped his defender, skated into the circle, and fired a wrist shot that snuck through Penguins goaltender Tom Barrasso. Just like that, the Blackhawks were on the board.

The Penguins had a chance to even up the score with a power play of their own, but they couldn't get the puck past Ed Belfour. To make things worse for the Penguins, they could not figure out how to handle Chicago's aggressive offense, as the Blackhawks scored two more goals in a short span of 26 seconds. The first of the two goals was scored by Michel Goulet after stealing the puck from a Chicago player in the offensive zone, and the second one was a rebound goal by Dirk Graham after Barrasso could not handle a shot from Chelios.

With just over six minutes left in the first period, the visiting Chicago Blackhawks had a three-goal lead, devastating the home crowd.

Thankfully for that crowd and the Penguins, Phil Bourque managed to score with two and a half minutes left in the first period. Ed Belfour had lost his stick and couldn't defend the wraparound shot from Bourque, which gave the Penguins a gasp of air.

That quick gasp of air was taken away early in the second period when Brent Sutter scored a goal following a two-on-one rush for the Blackhawks. Things were not looking good for the Penguins, but there was still time left on the clock.

With just over five minutes left in the second period, Rick Tocchet tallied a goal for the Penguins, making the score 4-2. One minute later, Mario Lemieux added another goal for the home team, and the score was 4-3 as the game moved into the third period.

Unlike the first two periods of the contest, the third period was played much more conservatively. Chicago tried to maintain the lead they had built up over the first and second periods, while the Penguins wanted to score at least one more without taking too many risks and allowing the Blackhawks to pressure them into mistakes.

The tension in the arena was high, and anxiety continued to build throughout the period. In moments like these, star players are called upon to make a difference when it matters. This time, the star player was Jaromir Jagr. After intercepting a pass from the Blackhawks in the offensive zone, Jagr began to skate and stickhandle, looking for a way through. Brent Sutter approached and tried to check Jagr, but he was too quick and stepped around Sutter toward the center of the ice. Another Chicago defender came out to challenge, but Jagr made another quick movement with the puck to avoid losing possession.

Critically, one of Jagr's teammates was tied up with the second Chicago defenseman in front of goalie, Ed Belfour, and because that teammate thought that Jagr was going to shoot through the screen, he jumped. That jump froze Ed Belfour for just a moment, he could not see Jagr cleanly through the screen, but for a moment, because he saw that Penguins player jump, he thought the shot was coming.

But it wasn't. Jagr carried the puck around the two screened players, and then shot. Belfour could not recover and get to a good position in his crease fast enough. As he shuffled over to cover the ground he'd lost while looking for the shot that wasn't coming, Jagr finally did shoot. The backhand shot slid through the legs of the goaltender, tying the game with just under five minutes left.

The Penguins had come all the way back from a devastating three-goal-hole. The game was tied, the arena was going nuts, and the momentum was squarely with the Penguins.

Then, with less than 20 seconds left, the unbelievable. The Penguins had a faceoff in Chicago's zone, and Lemieux won it back to Larry Murphy, who fired it at the net. Lemieux was circling back toward the net as the shot came in, so when Belfour kicked a rebound out into the slot, Mario Lemieux was there to fire it home, giving his team the 5-4 lead with less than 15 seconds left in the game.

Ed Belfour lay on the ice in disbelief for a moment, knowing the game had slipped away from his team. It was the kind of loss that many teams find it difficult to recover from and continue battling.

As it turns out, it was an omen for the series. The Pittsburgh Penguins went on to sweep the Chicago Blackhawks and win the Stanley Cup. Many people look back at Jaromir Jagr's spectacular individual effort and the spark it provided to his team in their moment of need, and they credit his skill as having saved the Penguins' season.

It's difficult to argue otherwise. If he had not delivered that masterful goal by beating three Blackhawks on his own, the Penguins' fate may have gone another way.

Regardless, one cannot argue that the moment Jagr's stick took that puck away, something quite incredible took place. Very few NHL players have ever been able to outmaneuver three opponents in a row, but Jagr did it, and he did it when his team needed him to do it.

## Did You Know?

1.  Chicago only lost two games in the 1992 playoffs before reaching the Finals.

2.  In fact, Chicago set an NHL record by winning 11 playoff games in a row during that run.

3.  The 1992 Cup was the last one presented by NHL President John Ziegler before Gary Bettman took over the duty as Commissioner.

4.  The Penguins engraved the name of Bob Johnson, their former head coach who had died of cancer in November of 1991, on the Stanley Cup when they won it again.

5.  The Penguins' names were the last ones added to the "shoulder" of the Stanley Cup.

6.  The Blackhawks would not return to the Cup Finals until 2010.

# CHAPTER 10:

## BOBBY ORR

It is rare for an NHL player active before 1980 to have an iconic image associated with their greatness. After all, pictures were not so easy to capture in the 1960s and 70s, and it's still difficult to get the full story from a single snapshot in time. However, one NHL legend by the name of Bobby Orr has such a picture, and you should know the incredible story behind it, along with the rest of his amazing career in the NHL.

Bobby was the grandson of a professional soccer player who had emigrated to Canada from Northern Ireland, and his father, Doug, was a promising young hockey player. However, Doug elected to join the Royal Canadian Navy to serve during World War II, which ended any hopes of a hockey career. Still, the athleticism continued to pass down the line, and Bobby displayed great skill on the ice at a very early age.

Even at five years old, his skating ability greatly exceeded that of his peers, and he always won races around the ice. From ages five to ten, Bobby played a wing position. However, when his coach, former NHL player Bucko McDonald, moved him to defense, he helped Bobby develop a full understanding of the ice. Even on defense, Bobby was always encouraged to use his speed and skill to contribute on offense when possible.

Bobby continued to grow, and it didn't take long before an NHL team took notice. In 1961, when Bobby had just turned 14, the Boston Bruins saw him playing at a youth tournament in Ontario, so they made regular visits to his family's home and paid $1,000 in Canadian dollars to sponsor his youth hockey team. Because of this time and commitment, Orr decided to sign with the Bruins one year later.

However, because Bobby was too young to play in the NHL, he needed to play for a junior league team. Undeterred, the Bruins made deals to own a second junior team, allowing them to keep hold of Orr's rights until he was old enough to sign.

When the time finally came for Orr to sign with the Bruins, he had the entire league buzzing with anticipation. He had dominated the junior leagues during his time there, and many figured that his impact on the NHL would be immediate.

Little did they know that he would have an impact on the game before even touching NHL ice! When offered a contract for US $8,000 and a signing bonus of $7,000, he and his agent counter-offered and even refused to play for a period of time, which he spent with Team Canada. Finally, the Bruins paid him an undisclosed amount, but many estimate it was between $25,000 and $40,000. It marked the first time a player had leveraged his position to get a better offer from league management, bringing agents into the mix.

Though the Bruins' first season with Bobby Orr on the roster was rough, as the team had a record of 17-43-10, Orr was earning the respect of players around the league, and attendance at Bruins games was up substantially. Orr won the Calder Trophy with 13 goals and 28 assists, which was significant as a defenseman in the league.

In his second season, despite playing only 46 games because of injuries, Orr was named an All-Star and went on to win the Norris Trophy as the league's best defenseman, an award that he would go on to win seven more times (in a row). The Bruins made the playoffs, but they were swept in the first round by the Montreal Canadiens, the team that would go on to win the Cup that year.

Two seasons later, in 1969, Orr began a campaign that will likely never be matched by a defenseman. At the end of the year, Bobby had accumulated 120 points, which was only six points away from the league record at the time. For that incredible performance, Orr was awarded the Art Ross Trophy as the NHL's top scorer. It was the first time the award had ever been earned by a defenseman, and no other defenseman in league history has been able to replicate the feat, except Orr himself. He even won the Hart Trophy as the league's regular season MVP. It was a great season for the defenseman, but it wasn't over yet.

More importantly, the Bruins were in the 1970 playoffs, and Orr continued to lead the way for his team.

In the opening series, the Boston Bruins took the first two home games against the New York Rangers, with Orr contributing two goals in Game 1. However, the Rangers held serve for their home games, winning both Games 3 and 4 to even the series. When the series shifted back to Boston, the Bruins held on to win a close 3-2 game, taking a 3-2 lead in the series.

For Game 6 in New York, the Rangers jumped out to a 1-0 lead after a power play goal in the first period from Brad Park. Orr notched a power play goal in the second period to tie the game, and the Bruins added one more to take a 2-1 lead heading into the third. Orr scored again in the third, and the Bruins pulled away to win the deciding game, 4-1.

In the second round, also the semifinals, the Bruins swept the Chicago Black Hawks, with Orr adding one goal to his team's dominant performance.

In the Stanley Cup Finals, the Bruins faced the St. Louis Blues. While many expected a close match, the Bruins never really let that happen. The only game of the series where the Blues stood a chance was Game 4, which went to overtime.

Down 3-0 in the series, the Blues needed a victory to extend the series and begin their comeback, but Bobby Orr and the Bruins were excited to raise the Cup as soon as possible. Forty seconds into the first overtime, Orr pinched in to keep the puck in the Blues zone, beating two St. Louis players as they thought the puck was coming out of the zone. If the puck had gotten by Orr in that moment, it would have been a two-on-one opportunity for the Blues. The hockey gods were kind, and Orr had possession, so he passed to Derek Sanderson, who was below the goal line in the corner. As Orr raced for the front of the net, he beat his defender to the crease just as Sanderson made a return pass to Orr.

Orr shot from close range, and because the goaltender had gone for a poke check, there was an opening between his pads for Orr's shot to squeak through. As he saw the puck go into the net, Orr jumped in celebration. Because he was being tripped by a St. Louis player during his jump, his body went parallel to the ice surface about four to five feet in the air before coming down. The iconic picture alluded to earlier perfectly captures Orr in mid-flight, having just won the Stanley Cup for the first time.

As his team celebrated their first championship since 1941, Bobby Orr was awarded the Conn Smythe Trophy as the MVP of the playoffs. He became the first player in NHL history to win the Art Ross, Hart, Norris, and Conn Smythe

Trophies in a single season, another record that has gone untouched ever since.

Bobby Orr's career would have a few more highlights, including another Stanley Cup in 1972, and a second Art Ross Trophy in 1975. He was inducted into the Hockey Hall of Fame in 1979, skipping the three-year waiting period, which made him the youngest player ever inducted at age 39.

For good measure, Orr helped Team Canada win gold at the 1976 Canada Cup, an international competition that was the first to allow both amateur and professional players to represent their countries, rather than only allowing amateurs, as the Olympics often did.

Many hockey fans and historians consider Bobby Orr to be the best defenseman in the history of the sport, and few rank him lower than third in the list of all-time greatest players in league history. His skill and speed were essential to how he played the game, and he used those assets to dominate the sport from the blueline as no other player has ever been able to emulate.

## Did You Know?

1. Orr won three consecutive Hart Trophies from 1975 to 1977.

2. Orr holds the record for best plus/minus in a single season with +124.

3. Bobby signed with the Black Hawks to play the 1976–77 season after knee surgery.

4. In his only international hockey tournament, Orr was named the Canada Cup MVP in 1976.

5. Orr's surgically repaired left knee was featured in a MasterCard commercial in 2008.

6. Bobby finished his career with more penalty minutes than points (953 to 915).

# CHAPTER 11:

## WAYNE GRETZKY

It wouldn't be a book about the most incredible hockey stories if "The Great One" was not included. After all, most would consider Wayne Gretzky to be the best to ever play the game, and for good reason. His career is littered with trophies and numerous records, many of which are considered untouchable in today's game. Some try to criticize and say that he played the sport when his competition was not as high in quality as today's players, but that would be selling him short. Let's take a look at the story and career of Wayne Gretzky, and maybe you'll come to appreciate just how great he was.

Wayne began playing hockey at the age of two when he would use a souvenir stick to shoot balls while his grandmother tended to the goal. It didn't take long for people around him to notice that he was different. By age six, Wayne was playing on a team against ten-year-old opponents and handling the puck better than most of them. While on that team, he had to wear a jersey that was sized for a ten-year-old boy, and because it was so baggy, he had to tuck it in on one side. It was something he continued to do throughout his entire career.

By the age of 13, it was estimated that Wayne had scored over 1,000 goals in organized play, and his hometown was pretty much sick of him dominating the hockey scene, overshadowing other kids and being the star every time he stepped on the ice. When he turned 14, Wayne's parents moved him to a big hockey city, Toronto, where he and his parents could escape the hometown pressures and give him a chance to expand his hockey skills.

In his first year with the Toronto Nationals in the Junior B league, Wayne scored 60 points in 28 games to win Rookie of the Year. Surprisingly, when the Ontario Major Junior Hockey League draft took place a year later with Gretzky eligible, he was selected third by the Sault Ste. Marie Greyhounds. It was with this team that he wore number 99 for the first time, another tradition he would carry forward through the rest of his hockey career. He wanted to wear nine for his favorite NHL player, Gordie Howe, but another player on the team already had that number.

After a season with the Greyhounds that featured 182 points in 64 games from Gretzky, he was signed by the Indianapolis Racers of the World Hockey Association. He was 17 at the time, and the NHL did not allow their teams to sign players under the age of 20. The WHA used this to their advantage to sign young, talented players to big contracts, all in an effort to save their league.

Gretzky scored his first professional goal in his fifth game, and he scored again four seconds later. But, after only eight games with the Racers, his rights were sold to another WHA team, the Edmonton Oilers. The Racers folded months later, and Gretzky would play the rest of the season in Edmonton, where he collected 104 points in 72 regular season games, then 20 more points in 13 playoff contests.

Gretzky's performance, along with other talented players in the WHA, convinced the NHL to allow four WHA teams to join the league, including Gretzky's Oilers.

With the league's expansion, some wondered if Gretzky would continue to find success in the NHL. After all, he was only 160 pounds, which was 30 pounds lighter than the league average. To no surprise, he made up for the size difference the same way he did in every other league: with skill and knowledge of the game.

In his first NHL season, Gretzky proved that he was the real deal. He finished the year with 137 points, tied for the league lead with Marcel Dionne, and won the Hart Trophy as the regular season MVP. He had become the youngest player to score 50 goals in a season, but he wasn't done. Not by a long shot.

For starters, he would go on to win seven more consecutive Hart Trophies, but let's not get ahead of ourselves. In his second season, he tallied 164 points. That included 102 assists, breaking a record held by Bobby Orr. He also notched five assists in the first game of the playoffs that year, which is also a record.

But because Wayne Gretzky was just that good, he refused to be outdone, even by himself. In his third NHL year, he set a personal best (and NHL record) with 92 goals to go with his 120 assists, for a total of 212 points.

To this point in his career, few would question whether Gretzky was the best active player in the league. However, there were questions about the team's playoff performances, which were not very strong in those early years. It wasn't for lack of trying on Wayne's part, either, as his scoring did not slow down in the postseason.

In his first year, the team played three playoff games, and Gretzky had three points. Pretty good for that era, but not outstanding. In his second year, the team played nine games, and Gretzky contributed 21 points. That is a stellar rate of scoring production, but the team could not come together around him. His third year, the 212-point season just mentioned, only saw the Oilers play five playoff games. Gretzky had 12 points.

No one was blaming Wayne Gretzky for the team's performance in the playoffs, but the worry was whether Wayne would continue to stick with the Oilers, or if he would flee for a winning team.

However, Wayne's loyalty was never in doubt when it came to the locker room. He was determined to win in Edmonton with the teammates he had grown so close to on the ice.

The 1983 playoffs featured the Oilers' first deep run in the NHL, and Gretzky was doing his part to contribute. In 16 playoff games, Wayne tallied 38 points. Unfortunately, the Oilers were swept in the Stanley Cup Finals by the dynastic New York Islanders.

It was the kind of disheartening defeat that can derail the careers of lesser players. However, Gretzky was determined to learn from the situation and come back even stronger. Finally, in the 1984 playoffs, the Oilers reached the pinnacle of the league, avenging their loss against the Islanders from the previous season. It was the first Stanley Cup of four for Gretzky, as the Oilers would win in 1985, '87, and '88 before another career-changing moment.

In a situation simply known in hockey history as "The Trade," Wayne Gretzky was traded to the Los Angeles Kings. It was a dramatic situation for the best player in the world, but he didn't allow the pain and hurt of leaving his only NHL team behind. In the city of Los Angeles, the arrival of "The Great One" helped grow the sport of hockey on the West Coast.

During his years with Los Angeles, he still collected over 100 points for five of those seasons. The team did not win the Stanley Cup during that time, but his contribution to the organization, and the game of hockey, was immense.

To round out his playing career, Gretzky played the end of one season, along with a playoff run, with the St. Louis Blues in 1996, then played three seasons with the New York Rangers before retiring.

Wayne Gretzky finished his NHL career with 2,857 points. He had 894 goals and 1,963 assists, numbers that many consider to be untouchable. Alexander Ovechkin may threaten the goal record, but the assists are legendary.

In total, he collected nine Hart Trophies, ten Art Ross Trophies, five Lady Byng Trophies, and the Lester B. Pearson Award five times. In the realm of hockey player statistics, Wayne Gretzky's accomplishments are the best in the history of the sport.

He also spent four seasons as the head coach of the Phoenix Coyotes, though the team struggled to post a winning record during any of those campaigns.

There are many great NHL players in every era of the game. So far, though, Wayne Gretzky remains a cut above the rest. Until another star learns to score at the rate Gretzky did, and then do it for 20 years, his incredible career will remain at the top of the list.

## Did You Know?

1.  Gretzky is the only player to tally more than 200 points in a season.

2.  Wayne is credited with making the sport of hockey popular in California after his trade to Los Angeles.

3.  The NHL retired his number, 99, for the whole league. No other player will ever wear it.

4.  Wayne was named an officer of the Order of Canada in 1984 for his contributions to the sport.

5.  Gretzky found out about the trade to Los Angeles two hours after his team had won the Stanley Cup in 1988.

6.  A year after being traded, Edmonton erected a statue of Gretzky outside of their arena.

# CHAPTER 12:

## THE MIRACLE ON MANCHESTER

There are many examples of the traditional David vs. Goliath matchups throughout hockey history, but very few of those stories have David pinned to the ground with Goliath's foot on his throat, going for the kill. This single hockey game, though, has all the dramatic moments required to become an incredible moment. Let's look at the particulars of this matchup; it'll be easy to see why the events that took place were so improbable.

First, the Edmonton Oilers entered the 1982 playoffs with 111 points in the regular season, making them the first seed in the Clarence Campbell Conference. The team was led on offense by Wayne Gretzky, who was on the verge of winning his third straight Hart Trophy as the league MVP. The team also featured star players such as Mark Messier, Jari Kurri, Paul Coffey, and Grant Fuhr.

It was a dominant roster that set NHL scoring records during that regular season. They scored 417 goals during that campaign, while the next closest team on the list scored 32 fewer. It also helped that the team had a better-than-average defense, giving up 26 fewer goals than the league average during the season.

On the other side of the ice, the Los Angeles Kings limped into the playoffs with 63 points, fewer than any other playoff team that year. The team even fired their coach halfway through the year to bring in a replacement. On offense, the squad scored 314 goals on the year, which was just under the league average, and their 369 goals against was the third worst in the league.

Marcel Dionne was their superstar, who was eighth in league scoring that year with 117 points. His linemate, Dave Taylor, had 106 points to his name, making them a formidable duo on the ice. Larry Murphy was their best defenseman, while the team's goaltenders struggled to keep pucks out of the net.

The two mismatched teams met eight times during the regular season, with the Oilers winning five, losing one, and tying two. In those contests, the Oilers scored 24 more goals than the Kings did.

In every aspect of the game, the Edmonton Oilers had the advantage. So, when these two teams met in the first round of the playoffs, few gave the Kings a chance. However, Los Angeles shocked the hockey world with a Game 1 victory in Edmonton, 10-8. Some thought that predicting a Kings upset victory in the series was premature after one game, especially after Edmonton bounced back in Game 2, winning in overtime to tie the series.

Game 3 was the first to take place in Los Angeles, and the home team's crowd was excited to get behind their players and inspire them to victory. When the puck dropped, though, the Oilers showed those fans that a victory was unlikely. Halfway through the first period, Mark Messier scored a goal after the Oilers killed off a penalty, swinging the early momentum heavily in favor of the visitors.

To make things worse, Wayne Gretzky himself added a shorthanded goal at the end of the first period, giving the Oilers a 2-0 lead heading into the second. The Kings had a chance, though, as they were still on the power play at the beginning of that second period. Did they take advantage of it?

Well, no. They did worse, allowing another shorthanded goal, this time from Lee Fogolin. The score was 3-0, and things looked quite miserable for the home team. A few minutes later, Risto Siltanen scored at even strength for the Oilers, making the score 4-0. Don't worry, there's more. Gretzky struck on the power play with just under six minutes left in the period, making the score 5-0, which left the crowd stunned and the Kings players dejected.

Into the third period, the Kings knew they had to find a way back if they wanted a chance to win the series. The winner of Game 3 would have a much better chance of winning the series, and with 20 minutes remaining, Los Angeles tried to mount a comeback.

A little over two minutes into the third, Jay Wells of the Kings got one back for the home team after sneaking a shot past a screened Grant Fuhr, making the score 5-1. The goal helped the Kings players believe they still had a chance, so their efforts improved. A few minutes later, they earned a power play and found paydirt when Doug Smith was able to score off a rebound in front of the net.

The two teams continued to battle as the clock ticked away. With under six minutes in the period, Charlie Simmer drove to the Oiler net with the puck, shooting from a sharp angle. Grant Fuhr made the save, but an Oilers' stick pushed Fuhr's pad, allowing the puck to cross the goal line. It was the break the Kings needed, and for the first time since the halfway point of the first period, the Los Angeles crowd was revitalized. They believed that their team could finish the comeback. Still, time was not on their side.

Then, with five minutes left in the game, Garry Unger of the Oilers was assessed a five-minute major for high sticking, meaning that Los Angeles would likely spend the rest of regulation on the power play. However, the Los Angeles player cut by the high stick also received a roughing penalty. The teams would play four-on-four until that penalty expired, and then the Kings would have the remaining three minutes of power play time.

During the four-on-four, Steve Bozek and Mark Hardy drove into the Oiler zone two-on-two against the Oilers' defense and crisscrossed, with Bozek dropping the puck to Hardy during the switch. Hardy then moved around

Gretzky and fired a shot that caught Fuhr off guard. Hardy's shot found the back of the net, the crowd went wild, and the clock still had four minutes.

Then, a chance for the Oilers to regain the momentum presented itself. Oilers forward Pat Hughes collected a loose puck at center ice and raced down for a breakaway. Mario Lessard made the save, then caught the rebound attempt from Hughes to end the play. It was a big moment, but it also represented the trouble that the Kings were having when trying to establish pressure on the power play.

With a minute and a half left, the Kings' coaching staff used an old NHL rule to their advantage. Whenever a team elects to pull their goaltender for poor performance, replacing him with a backup, the backup player coming onto the ice is granted a minute or two of warmup shots. It was basically being abused to get teams an extra timeout.

The Kings used this strategy to help their first power play unit get a rest for the final push to tie the game. Then, with just over a minute left in the game, they pulled their goaltender entirely, giving their team a six-on-four advantage. Marcel Dionne got possession of the puck down low in the Oilers zone, spinning away from defenders and looking for an opening. Then Simmer retrieved an attempted pass from Dionne and rotated into the corner before trying to move the puck behind the net.

At that moment, Dionne got free, and Simmer fed him the puck in the slot. Dionne's shot was saved by Fuhr, and the rebound went back to the corner where Gretzky tried to clear, but it was taken away by Jim Fox of the Kings with less than ten seconds left. Fox stickhandled back toward the middle of the ice before passing the puck back to the blue line, where Mark Hardy was waiting.

With seven seconds left on the clock, Hardy flung the puck toward the net as Oilers players desperately tried to block the attempt. The puck got through, forcing Fuhr to make a pad save, but the rebound fell onto the stick of Steve Bozek in the slot, who quickly shot the rebound past Fuhr and into the net with five seconds left in regulation.

The building exploded in cheers. The Kings tied the game, 5-5.

As the pandemonium unfolded, the Oilers players on the ice were stunned. A couple of them remained down on the ice, exhausted and in disbelief at what had just taken place. It truly was a miracle comeback, but overtime remained.

Early in that overtime session, Lessard mishandled a bouncing puck and had to slide out to try and keep possession for his team. When he slid out, the puck bounced off his pad and onto the stick of Mark Messier, who coolly skated around Lessard and attempted a backhand shot toward the net. However, that goal was defended by two

Kings players instead of their goaltender, and Messier's shot was forced wide, hitting the boards behind the goal, which allowed Lessard to recover without costing his team the game.

A minute later, during a faceoff in the Oilers' zone, Doug Smith won the draw back to Daryl Evans, who immediately fired a slapshot toward Fuhr. The shot was moving too quickly for Fuhr to react, and in an instant, the Los Angeles Kings had completed their comeback against the Edmonton Oilers. It was a dramatic victory for the underdog team.

After this incredible hockey game, the series continued with an Oilers victory in Game 4, but a Kings victory in the deciding Game 5. Gretzky, Messier, and the Oilers were eliminated. Los Angeles would lose in the next round to the Vancouver Canucks, but the Miracle on Manchester victory is a storied moment in the team's history. On the 40th anniversary of the event, the team revealed a retro jersey inspired by the sweaters worn during that fateful day.

Of course, the Kings would have fewer bright spots for another decade, while the Oilers would go on to win five championships over the next eight years. Still, the Los Angeles team demonstrated that an incredible hockey moment is always possible, no matter the odds or the opponent. Just keep digging until the final horn sounds!

## Did You Know?

1. The Miracle on Manchester is the biggest comeback in playoff history.

2. The Kings' owner, Jerry Buss, left the game early when it looked like the Kings were going to be embarrassed.

3. After Vancouver defeated Los Angeles, they would go on to be swept by the Islanders in the Finals.

4. The Los Angeles Kings continued to struggle until they traded for Gretzky a few years later.

5. The Kings have won two Stanley Cups, in 2012 and 2014.

6. Gretzky had 12 points in the series, but the Oilers still lost.

# CHAPTER 13:

## THE MICHIGAN GOAL
## AND THE FORSBERG

Few moments in hockey history have become a worldwide phenomenon, with players of all ages and skills attempting to replicate what they just learned was possible on the ice. When a moment like that comes along, usually once a generation if at all, it should be celebrated and properly understood. After all, if you want to be the biggest hockey fan in the world, you should know how the best moves and moments came to be. This chapter focuses on two specific goals, one scored by a college player during the 1996 NCAA hockey regional semifinals, and another scored by one of the most prolific players in the NHL.

Let's set the stage between the two college teams playing back in 1996 when the first legendary goal was scored for the first time. The Michigan Wolverines are facing off against the Minnesota Golden Gophers in the second round of the NCAA tournament. The Wolverines of this year were a stacked squad, with 11 future NHL players on the team. The team won more than 30 games during the season, making them one of the favorites to make a deep run in the tourney.

The Golden Gophers were a team that had been getting stronger throughout the year, and they felt confident that they would have a chance to beat Michigan if they met in the tournament. In fact, earlier that season, Minnesota had defeated Michigan during a Thanksgiving tournament.

When the two teams met in that second-round matchup, with a chance to go to the Frozen Four on the line, Minnesota was doing well. They found themselves with a 2-1 lead in the second period, but Michigan had a power play with a chance to tie the game.

During that power play, though, the Golden Gophers were playing well defensively, effectively tying up the puck along the boards to kill precious seconds off the clock and inch closer to regaining their penalized player.

Then, when Michigan player Mike Legg found himself behind the net with the puck, defenders guarding his teammates and the front of the net from any close-range chances, Legg took a risk. Using a trick that many young hockey players try in practice, Legg laid the face of his stick blade down on the puck, then curled his stick around, lifting the puck off the ice to rest on his stick blade. With the puck sitting on the blade, Legg simply reached his stick around to the front of the net and deposited the puck into the top corner of the goal. The Minnesota goaltender had not seen Legg put the puck onto his stick, so he assumed the wraparound attempt was coming along the ice and did not cover the top of the net.

The goal counted, the fans cheered, and the commentators were confused until they saw the replay of what had happened. It was groundbreaking for a player to attempt something like that during a competitive game. Some reflected that if Legg's move had failed, he would have likely been punished by his coaches for the foolishness. Instead, his goal sparked his team. The Michigan Wolverines would go on to win the game and the tournament, but that is a footnote to what happened in the world of hockey after the goal.

That night, video of the goal that would come to be known as the "Michigan" goal or the "lacrosse" goal was on every news and sports network across the continent. Within a matter of days, players of all ages began practicing the move, and over time, their practice paid off on bigger and bigger stages around the world.

Sidney Crosby, one of the best to ever play the game, scored using the move in a minor league game in 2003. Robert Nilsson performed the feat during his time in the AHL back in 2006. Nils Hoglander even used the move to score a goal during the World Junior Championships in 2019. Andrei Svechnikov, as a member of the Carolina Hurricanes, has used the move on multiple occasions to score goals at the NHL level.

That is not a complete list of players who have accomplished the feat, but you get the idea. This move has become so well known that it is even featured in hockey video games. Video game players can now use the move to score from behind the net in their favorite digital arena.

Now, let's switch gears to a goal that made international news on one of the biggest stages in the world. After all, the goal scored by Mike Legg during the NCAA tournament in 1996 was great, but there is one goal that happened during a much bigger moment, with so much more on the line.

The year is 1994. The Winter Olympics are taking place in Lillehammer, Norway. The men's ice hockey tournament, in particular, is garnering quite a bit of attention as Team Canada outperformed expectations and made it to the gold medal game, where they were facing Team Sweden.

During this time for Olympic competitions, professional athletes, those paid to play in the best leagues in the world, were not permitted to compete in the Olympics, which are considered to be amateur competitions. This often means that most countries will have rosters of players that are much younger than the average professional team because those skilled youngsters haven't yet been signed to a professional team.

This also means that stars can be born on the biggest stage in the world, and that is pretty much what happened during this gold medal game. The two teams battled hard in the early going, but it was Sweden who struck first with a goal from Tomas Jonsson on the power play. What followed was more than two full periods of scoreless hockey as Canada spent much of the game being hemmed into their own zone.

The Canadians were heavily outshot for most of the game, but as the contest moved into the third period, they knew they had to push offensively to tie the score. Then, with less than 11 minutes left in the game, Paul Kariya scored for Team Canada. Even more of a shock, Derek Mayer scored for the Canadians a little over two minutes later. Suddenly, the Swedes were behind by one with eight minutes left.

Team Sweden dug in and continued to dominate the game offensively, but the clock continued to tick as the favorites looked for an equalizer of their own. Then, with under two minutes left in the game, Magnus Svensson scored another power-play goal for Team Sweden, tying the game and forcing overtime to decide the gold medal winners.

Except, overtime wasn't enough. The two teams played ten minutes of golden goal overtime hockey with no result, meaning that the game would have to be decided by a penalty shootout. Each team would get five shooters, and whichever team scored the most goals would win gold.

The Canadians made their first two attempts, while Sweden only made one. With the next three shooters for each team, only Peter Forsberg made his attempt. This meant that after five shooters for each team, the score was still tied. When a shootout is tied after five shooters, the format changes. Each team would send one player to shoot until one team scores in their attempt and the other team misses. If both teams score or miss, another single round takes place until the winner is decided.

During the first set of extra shooters, both goaltenders were up to the task. But, in the seventh round of the shootout, the second extra shooter for each team set to shoot, Peter Forsberg, who had scored in the fourth round of the shootout already, was set to shoot again for Sweden.

This time, though, instead of using the deke he'd used the first time, he tried something new. With the gold medal on the line, he used a move that he had only used one time before in the Swedish League. As he skated down on the Canadian goaltender Corey Hirsch, Forsberg faked a shot as he skated to his left. But, as Hirsch moved with him to the left, Forsberg shifted his hands, stick, and puck back to his right, leaning across Hirsch with one hand on his stick to guide the puck just out of the reach of Hirsch's sprawling body and into the open net.

The crowd was stunned by the move. The commentators thought it was unplanned, but Forsberg had done it intentionally. The Swedes won the gold medal on the very next play when Paul Kariya could not score for Canada. It was a legendary moment in the world of hockey, and just like the Michigan goal, players at every level began to practice the Forsberg move. It has been completed at the NHL level many times, and it is always referred to as "The Forsberg."

It was such a big moment in the country of Sweden that they even made a commemorative stamp of the moment. However, if you look closely at that stamp, you'll notice that the goaltender pictured is wearing a different jersey color and number because Canadian goaltender Corey Hirsch did not give the country permission to use his likeness in the image.

Both goals, the Forsberg and Michigan, have had significant impacts on the game of hockey. They have both inspired creativity from players of all ages, as well as changed the way the game is played. Goaltenders and defenders must be aware of these new possibilities.

These incredible moments in hockey history have changed the course of the game permanently. What great move will be the next cultural icon?

## Did You Know?

1. When Forsberg first tried his new move in the Swedish league, his attempt failed.

2. Some contend that Mike Legg learned the lacrosse goal technique from Bill Armstrong, a player who only played one game with the Flyers but used the strategy in the AHL.

3. It was 23 years between Mike Legg's goal and the first NHL player to accomplish the lacrosse goal.

4. Tyler Ennis was likely the first player to attempt the Michigan in an NHL game, in 2016–17.

5. Forsberg learned his patented move from Kent Nilsson, who played from 1976 to 1998.

6. Forsberg set a record when he scored 31 points in seven games during the 1993 World Junior Championships.

# CHAPTER 14:

## MARTIN BRODEUR

There have been great NHL goaltenders throughout the history of the game, but very few have demonstrated a unique knowledge of the game the way that Martin Brodeur did during his career. Let's look at the incredible career of this impressive goaltender and examine how he was able to find such success at the highest level of the sport.

As a child, Martin Brodeur played hockey as a forward, but after serving as the team's backup for a tournament, his coach asked him if he wanted to switch positions for good. At seven years old, it was likely a difficult decision, but it was a decision that would end up changing the course of hockey history.

For the next few years, Martin seemed to enjoy the new position. When he was 12, though, he almost quit playing the sport altogether after being removed from his team's starting lineup for missing a game. Thankfully, one of Martin's brothers was able to convince him to stick with it.

As Martin entered his teenage years, he began to train in several different styles of goaltending. Looking back, Brodeur credits his success to understanding the strengths and weaknesses of different goaltending strategies, allowing him to play a hybrid style that helped him dominate the game.

As young Brodeur learned these styles and became a true student of the position, he reached the Quebec Major Junior

League, making the All-Rookie team in 1990. Following that one season in juniors, Brodeur was drafted 20th overall by the New Jersey Devils that summer. He continued to play in the junior league for two more seasons, though he did play four games for the Devils during the 1991–92 season. He won his first game in the NHL when the Devils beat the Bruins 4-2.

Then, Brodeur spent the 1992–93 season in the American Hockey League with the Utica Devils, and although he did not post spectacular numbers, he was still called upon to be the team's starting goaltender during the 1993–94 season. What followed was nothing short of incredible. In that opening season, he won the Calder Trophy as the best rookie in the NHL, helping the Devils to the second-best record in the league. His team also reached the Eastern Conference Finals, where they fell one game short of reaching the Stanley Cup Finals.

However, it didn't take long for Brodeur and the Devils to return to the playoffs. In the lockout-shortened 1994–95 season, Brodeur and his team finished fifth in their conference to reach the playoffs, where they found another gear. In the first round, they defeated the Boston Bruins, and Brodeur had three shutouts out of the four victories. The second round also featured a strong defensive performance, as Brodeur only surrendered nine goals over the course of five games.

The Philadelphia Flyers went down in six games, then the Devils swept the Detroit Red Wings, allowing only seven goals over those four games. In his second season in the league, Brodeur helped the Devils capture a Stanley Cup.

The following season, Brodeur set a league record for minutes played by a goaltender in a single season, but the Devils just barely missed the playoffs. Still looking to add to his resume, Brodeur had the lowest goals-against average by any goaltender in nearly 30 years. During the first round against Montreal, Brodeur scored a goal on his own, firing the puck the length of the ice into the open net to secure a Game 1 victory. It was the first time an NHL goaltender had scored a goal in the playoffs.

His next big accomplishment came during the 1999–2000 season, when he won 43 regular season games for the second time in his career, leading the Devils to fourth place in the Eastern Conference, just two points behind the Flyers. In the first round of the playoffs, Brodeur's hybrid style of goaltending came to life again, smothering the Florida Panthers by only allowing six goals in four games.

In the second round, Brodeur notched two shutouts against the Toronto Maple Leafs as the Devils advanced in six games. In the Eastern Conference Finals, it was another matchup against their rivals, the Philadelphia Flyers. Things didn't go well for the Devils in the first four games, as the

Flyers jumped out to a 3-1 series lead with a chance to advance to the Stanley Cup Finals with one more win.

However, Brodeur and the Devils decided they'd had enough, and just as he had in so many previous playoff series, Martin Brodeur shut the door on the Flyers. Over the next three games, Brodeur gave up one goal per game, and the Devils fought back to win the series and advance to the Stanley Cup Finals.

This time, the Devils were facing the Dallas Stars, a strong team in the Western Conference, but a squad that finished with fewer regular season points than the Devils. After a high-scoring first game of the series, Brodeur did his thing once again by only allowing six goals in the next five games. The New Jersey Devils captured their second championship with Brodeur in goal.

For the 2000–2001 season, Brodeur struggled a bit during the regular season, statistically, but he still earned 40 wins for the third time in his career. As a result, the Devils earned the top seed in their conference. With four shutouts in the playoffs, the Devils marched to the Stanley Cup Finals once more, but they were defeated by the Colorado Avalanche in seven games.

At this point, many would consider Brodeur's career a success, but he was far from done making an impact on the league. In fact, he still had stats to build up and NHL rules to change. If that second one was unexpected, then it's time to look at the two NHL rules associated with Brodeur.

First, at the start of the 2005–06 season, the NHL drew a trapezoid shape behind each goal line, indicating that goaltenders could not handle the puck in the corners of their own zone. This rule was intended to put more pressure on defenses skating back to retrieve the puck, which the league hoped would increase scoring. Many people around the league believed that Brodeur was a target of this rule because he would often skate to the corners to play pucks dumped into the zone, helping his defense in the process.

It didn't help that one of the biggest proponents of the rule was the Flyers' former general manager, Bobby Clarke.

The second rule change came during the 2008 playoffs when the Devils were facing off against the New York Rangers. In that bitterly contested series, Rangers forward Sean Avery used a strange technique to try and screen Brodeur during a five-on-three advantage.

A typical NHL player will attempt to screen the goaltender by standing in front of the goal with their back to the goal, allowing them to see the play and react to any situation that might require them to move to one side or another.

However, because Avery's team had two extra skaters on the ice, he did not feel the need to face the play. Instead, he faced Brodeur and waved his stick and gloves in Brodeur's face, attempting to distract him from the play. The day after this game was played, the NHL announced that the behavior demonstrated by Avery would be penalized under the unsportsmanlike conduct rules from now on.

Overall, Brodeur ended his NHL career as one of the most decorated goaltenders in the history of the sport. He made nine All-Star teams to go with his three Stanley Cups. He was also awarded four Vezina Trophies as the best goaltender in the league. The William M. Jennings Trophy, which is given to the goaltender with the fewest goals allowed in a season (with a minimum of 25 games played), was also presented to Brodeur five different times.

Brodeur has the most wins all-time among goaltenders, with 691, and the next closest on the list is 140 behind. He also has the most shutouts of any goaltender in history, with 125. It helped that he played 1,266 regular season games, also a record of more than 200. It was a dominant career full of success and surprise, and it is why Martin Brodeur's story should be considered an incredible one by any hockey fan.

## Did You Know?

1. Brodeur's three goals are the most by any goaltender in league history.

2. He is the only goaltender with eight 40-win campaigns.

3. Brodeur missed 16 weeks of the 2008–09 season with a torn biceps tendon, one of the few injuries of his career.

4. A statue of Brodeur was erected outside of the Devils' arena in 2016.

5. He was a Vezina nominee nine times, but only won the award four times.

6. Brodeur was also nominated for the Hart Trophy three times.

# CHAPTER 15:

## PAVEL DATSYUK REVOLUTIONIZED HOCKEY CREATIVITY

NHL players, like most athletes, are trained in very strict regimens. They learn patterns, so when they are in stressful situations, their bodies do not fail them. However, some NHL players grow up learning the game quite differently, so when they make it to the best league in the world, they make little adjustments that tend to keep their opponents confused. One of the most revolutionary players in this regard is Pavel Datsyuk. This is a player who did not dominate the league on the stats sheets, but his unique way of playing the game was entertaining to fans and players around the league.

Let's see what made him so special.

Pavel Datsyuk was a smaller player who grew up in Russia playing hockey and soccer. In his teen years, he began playing for a minor league team in Russia, but he was overlooked by NHL scouts because he lacked the size necessary to be successful in the North American game. For this reason, Datsyuk went undrafted for the first two years he was eligible.

Then, in 1998, with the 171st pick, he was selected by the Detroit Red Wings. The team had a habit of selecting Russian and other European-born players because of their skill and speed, and while Datsyuk was not the fastest player, he did show an aptitude to play well on both sides of the puck.

When Datsyuk first hit the ice for Detroit during the 2001–2002 season, he had the privilege of playing alongside several future Hall-of-Fame players like Brett Hull, Luc Robitaille, Brendan Shanahan, Steve Yzerman, and Nick Lidstrom. It also helped that the Red Wings had a few great Russian players on the roster, including Igor Larionov and Sergei Fedorov. With an amazing roster around him, Datsyuk began to learn the North American game, and how he could manipulate it.

It didn't take long for Pavel Datsyuk to make his mark on the NHL, and he nearly helped the Wings win one of the biggest games of the season. During the 2002 Stanley Cup Finals, the Red Wings were playing against the Carolina Hurricanes. The teams split the first two games, and Game 3 was headed to overtime.

During the overtime, Datsyuk found himself with a little bit of space coming into the Carolina zone, and he was able to beat two of the Carolina defensemen by himself. With only the Carolina goaltender between him and victory, Datsyuk made a deke and tried to slip the puck between the legs of the goalie, only for the very tip of the goalie's pad stopping the puck and ending the play.

The Red Wings would go on to win that game, and the Stanley Cup, but it was an early flash showing that Datsyuk was a skillful player. He would often make passes other players couldn't see, or he would trick defenders with his shifting feet and artful stickhandling.

One move put him centerstage in the league. It would become known as his patented shootout move, one which other players would try to emulate later. It is a bit complicated to explain, but it is worth the trouble. When a player is skating on a breakaway and plans to shoot, one of the telltale signs is that the player will lift their off-foot before releasing the shot, because they are leaning forward over their stick to get more torque.

Datsyuk learned to mimic this movement, which, by itself, is not special. Players learn how to do this fake shot at a young age. However, Datsyuk stunned the hockey world with what he added to the move. When a player lifts one foot off the ice, it becomes difficult for that player to change the direction in which they are moving. Datsyuk learned that he could angle his left foot, the one still on the ice, to his right, thereby allowing him to drag the puck to the side.

Opposing goaltenders, seeing the right foot come off the ice, would think a shot was coming and go down into the butterfly. Datsyuk would wait for this commitment, then drag the puck around and shoot into what was often an open net left behind. The move was so advanced that many casual fans didn't understand what was happening. Pavel knew what the goalies were looking for, so he gave it to them and then fooled them into reacting.

With a few more successful seasons, Pavel Datsyuk's game only became stronger. He cooked up new ways to beat his opponents, and one of his favorite moves was the fake drop pass. When breaking out of his own zone, Datsyuk would curl around the boards to receive or pick up the puck. If an opponent was curling with him to attack or skate up the ice, Datsyuk would move his stick over the puck as if to drop it back to a waiting teammate. The defender would see the stick movement and attempt to intercept the pass, except the pass would never be made. Datsyuk would barely move the puck at all and instead would use a burst of speed to take advantage of the split-second hesitation from his opponent.

He would also find ways to slip through defenders who seemed like they had him lined up for a big hit. On more than one occasion, he caused opponents to hit each other when they thought they would be hitting him.

His most impressive moment, though, came during the 2014 playoffs when the Red Wings were up against a strong Boston Bruins team. Late in the third period, the game remained scoreless as both teams looked for the goal that just might win the game. Datsyuk and his teammates were heading out of their own zone. Johan Franzen had the puck along the boards and tried to flip it over to Datsyuk as he was skating up the middle. However, the pass was behind Datsyuk, making him have to reach back for it.

At this moment, three Boston players saw Datsyuk reaching back for the poor pass, so they all turned and prepared to swipe the puck away. However, Datsyuk barely got his stick on the puck and was able to drag it up to himself and away from the three attackers who thought they had a free turnover. As Datsyuk brought the puck across the blue line and into the Boston zone, his teammate, Justin Abdelkader, skated toward the net to occupy one of the Boston defensemen. Datsyuk fired a low wrist shot through the legs of that defender, and before goalie Tuukka Rask could react, the puck was under his arm and in the net.

It was always little moments like this one that NHL fans would appreciate, but Datsyuk also accomplished a lot of the more traditional milestones on the ice. To go along with the Stanley Cup, that he won as a rookie in 2002, Datsyuk helped the Red Wings capture another championship in 2008.

Statistically, he ended his career with the Red Wings with 918 total points, good enough for seventh place on the Red Wings all-time list. As far as trophies go, he also collected quite a few. He won the Lady Byng Memorial Trophy four times, and the Frank J. Selke Trophy three times. In 2017, he was selected as one of the 100 Greatest NHL Players by the league.

Internationally, Datsyuk represented his home country of Russia on many occasions, including for a gold medal victory during the 2018 Olympic Games. He also won gold with his team during the 2012 World Championships.

After his time in the NHL came to an end, Datsyuk played five seasons in the Russian super league, where his creativity was also celebrated by players and fans alike. His team won the league championship in 2017, and he was awarded an award for being the top veteran player of the league in 2021, the last year he played.

Pavel Datsyuk never claimed any scoring titles or MVP awards, but he was known around the league for being one of the most skilled players to ever touch the ice. He showed generations of young players what was possible, and many believe that today's league is more creative because of his play. That is an incredible feat.

## Did You Know?

1. In interviews, Datsyuk said his puck-handling skills came from practicing with lots of other kids, but they only had one puck to fight over.

2. The Red Wings traded Datsyuk's contract to the Coyotes in 2016, after he had left to play in Russia.

3. Datsyuk served as the captain of Team Russia for the 2014 Olympics.

4. Datsyuk won the Plus-Minus Award during the 2008 NHL season.

5. An NHL Player's Poll named Datsyuk the Smartest Player, and the Hardest to Take the Puck from.

6. Datsyuk was a four-time NHL All-Star and a two-time KHL All-Star.

# CHAPTER 16:

## HAYLEY WICKENHEISER

In modern times, with women receiving more and more respect from society, it is important to look back on the women who helped the movement before it was a cultural trend to do so. Even today, some people might put forward the age-old argument: "Women can't compete with men."

Now, regardless of your personal beliefs, if you are a fan of ice hockey, then you should know the name Hayley Wickenheiser, as well as the contributions that she has made to women's hockey. After all, there are few players in the world as decorated as she is. Plus, she has accomplished what no other woman has, but we'll save that key detail until we get to it. For now, let's see how Hayley got her start in hockey, and just how far she traveled down that path.

As a child, Hayley only played youth hockey on boys' teams. From the age of five to 13, she had known nothing else. Having that level of competition day in and day out can help a young player develop - if they don't quit. Hayley did not quit. As she moved into her teenage years, she played minor hockey in Calgary and represented the province of Alberta at the 1991 Canada Winter Games. Hayley scored the winning goal of the tournament, and she was named the gold medal game MVP.

With that performance, Hayley captured the attention of the National Team, and they added her to the roster when she was 15 years old in 1994. At her very first international competition, the 1994 World Championships, she only tallied one assist, but Team Canada brought home the gold.

It was an underwhelming beginning, but she was only getting started. Three years later, Team Canada would win another World Championship, and this time, Wickenheiser, now 18, earned a spot on the tournament All-Star team.

She was also finding success at the professional level, as she earned her first MVP for the Esso women's hockey nationals at age 17. While her team did not win that year, she was victorious with the Edmonton Chimos and the Calgary Oval X-Treme in the next two tournaments, where she also won MVP in each of those contests. Wickenheiser would continue to play for Calgary, including the inaugural season of the Western Women's Hockey League in 2004.

However, before that venture started, she had another goal in mind. Harkening back to her beginning years as a hockey player, she wanted to prove that she could handle herself with men. In this effort, Wickenheiser traveled to Europe, as the European game tended to be less violent and played with more skill. She was originally destined for the Italian league, but the sports federation in charge of the hockey league in Italy determined that women were not eligible to compete on men's teams. Phil Esposito even offered her a spot on the Cincinnati Cyclones of the ECHL, but she declined, not wanting to play on the smaller ice surfaces in North America.

After a lot of negotiating, Wickenheiser found a spot in a semi-professional Finnish league, called the HC Suomi-sarja. It's the third tier of hockey in Finland, so while it wasn't the highest level of men's hockey, she still held her own. In 23 games in her debut with HC Salamat, Wickenheiser notched two goals and added ten assists, a strong showing. It also marked the first time a woman had scored a goal in a men's semi-professional league.

While she was playing in various professional leagues in North America and Europe, she continued to represent Team Canada on the international stage. At her first Olympic Games in 1998, Wickenheiser played six games and collected eight points as Canada won silver. Over the next 18 years, Wickenheiser would compete with Team Canada in four more Olympic tournaments, and ten more World Championship tourneys. At the end of her international career, Hayley Wickenheiser had collected 38 World Championship goals and 46 assists, totaling 74 points in 56 games played. On the Olympic side of things, she had played 26 games, tallying 18 goals and 33 assists, for a total of 51 points, almost two points per game.

With Wickenheiser on the team, Canada never finished worse than second place. She has four Olympic gold medals and one silver medal to go along with seven golds and five silvers from the World Championships. It was an international career of greatness that will likely never be matched.

In 2010, Wickenheiser went to college and played collegiate hockey for the Calgary Dinos. Even though she was not the typical age of a college student, she had not used up her years of collegiate eligibility, so she played while she studied medicine. In those four years at the University of Calgary, she scored 55 goals in 68 games.

When one looks at the success she had on a men's team, along with the great leadership she showed at the collegiate level, and her accomplishments on the international stage, it is easy to see why Hayley Wickenheiser has had such a massive impact on women's hockey around the world. She demonstrated to every young girl that it is possible to compete with the boys. It takes a lot of determination and effort, but it is possible. She also was not done.

Wickenheiser retired from playing professional hockey to continue studying medicine, and she finished her family medicine residency in 2023. She was also hired as the assistant director of player development for the Toronto Maple Leafs of the NHL, and after almost three years in that post, she was promoted to the senior director of player development for the Leafs. She assists the younger players to develop into NHL-level talent, another layer of help she has provided to the game.

At every level she has played, Hayley Wickenheiser has found success on the ice. Her incredible story is worth remembering today because the impact she has made will ripple into the future for years to come.

## Did You Know?

1. Hayley Wickenheiser's full career spanned from 1993 to 2017.

2. She also played softball for Team Canada at the 2000 Summer Olympics.

3. Her hometown named its new recreation center after her in 2011.

4. Hayley wrote *Gold Medal Diary – Inside the World's Greatest Sports Event.*

5. She founded an event called WickFest, which showcases girls' and women's hockey players from all over the world.

6. She was one of the first women to have her likeness included in the *NHL* series of video games by EA Sports.

# CHAPTER 17:

## GORDIE HOWE'S LONG CAREER

Modern NHL players would consider a career of ten or more years to be a success. If an NHL player reaches 20 years, they are considered a legend. Those numbers, though, do not hold up very well against the storied career of the player they call "Mr. Hockey." Gordie Howe is widely regarded as one of the best to ever play the game, and it helps that he played for several more seasons than most other players. Let's see the incredible career of Gordie Howe and all the success he enjoyed over those decades on the ice.

From the age of eight, Gordie Howe was on the ice, playing hockey. By the age of 16, he left his hometown to pursue his hockey career, just one year after being invited to a training camp with the New York Rangers. He declined to sign with that team because it would have required a year at Notre Dame. Instead, a year later, he decided to sign with the Detroit Red Wings and join their junior team in Galt, Ontario.

After one year of limited playing time, he was promoted to the minor leagues, the Omaha Knights of the United States Hockey League. At 17 years old, he scored 48 points in 51 games with the Knights. With a stat line like that, it was no surprise when Howe was called up to the Detroit Red Wings when he was 18 years old. Of course, making his debut on October 16, 1946, Howe scored a goal in his very first NHL game.

From there, the sky was the limit. Although he was a talented player on offense, he had a habit of fighting a little too often. It was almost a tradition for established NHL players to fight the rookies and teach them to respect their elders, in a sense, but Howe would never shy away from a challenge.

Because of this penchant for fighting, the "Gordie Howe Hat Trick" became a fun statistic named after him. To achieve one of these hat tricks, a player needs to score a goal, tally an assist, and get a fighting major penalty all in one game. Howe himself only accomplished the feat twice in his career, oddly enough.

With all of that fighting, though, came risk. As Howe was showing the rest of the league how much of a threat he was, as he continued to improve every season, he suffered a scary injury during the 1950 playoffs when he tried to check Maple Leafs captain Ted Kennedy into the boards. The collision resulted in Howe sustaining a fractured skull, along with a broken nose and cheekbone.

With an injury like that, many players might consider it a wrap, that hockey is not worth the risk. Gordie Howe responded by returning the next season and playing in all 82 games for Detroit. Not only did he play in every game. He also led the league in scoring with 86 points, 20 more than the next closest player on the list.

To make sure the league knew who he was, Howe led the league in scoring for the next three years, becoming the first NHL player to successfully defend his scoring title more than once.

With Howe on the roster from 1946 to 1971, the Red Wings enjoyed several years of success. The team won four Stanley Cups with him on the team. Howe himself won six Art Ross Trophies as the player with the most points in the league. He also led the league in goals five times, and he won the league MVP six times.

Even more impressive is that Howe had his best scoring season at the age of 40, when he surpassed 100 points for the first and only time in his career, thanks in part to the expanded league, as well as his talented teammates, Alex Delvecchio, and Frank Mahovlich.

At the end of his NHL career in 1971, the Red Wings gave Howe a position in the front office of the team, and one year later, retired his number in the rafters of their arena.

However, even though he had played 25 years with the Red Wings and had to retire due to a chronic wrist issue, he still had the itch to play. Thankfully, that chance came along when the Houston Aeros of the World Hockey Association offered him a contract after signing both of Gordie's sons to the team. It was an easy decision for Gordie, as he did not find his position with the Red Wings to be worthwhile or meaningful.

What followed was two years of WHA championship victories and an MVP award for Gordie. He played a total of four seasons with the Aeros, and he reached 100 points in two of those seasons before he and his sons moved to the New England Whalers.

During one game when Marty Howe's cheekbone was broken by an opponent, Gordie returned the favor in the next game by cross-checking that same player in the face. Even in his late 40s, Gordie Howe did not shy away from confrontation on the ice.

As it happened, during the offseason after the 1978–79 season, the World Hockey Association folded, and the New England Whalers became the Hartford Whalers of the NHL. Gordie was back in the league where he had already played 25 years, but he was not ready to retire. In his one season with Hartford, Gordie tallied 41 points in 80 games. Because that last season ended in 1980, Gordie Howe played professional hockey in the 1940s, 50s, 60s, 70s, and 80s.

For good measure, Gordie played one game with the Detroit Vipers of the International Hockey League during their 1997–98 season.

It was a bit of a gimmick, sure, but it officially made Gordie Howe the only player to ever play professional hockey across six decades. It is a record that will likely last for quite a long time.

After reaching the second end of his professional hockey career, Gordie Howe collected many records, some of which still stand today. He holds the record for most games played with a single NHL team, as he played 1,687 games with the Red Wings.

Between the NHL and WHA regular season and playoff games, he played 2,421 games. He is tied with Chris Chelios with 26 NHL seasons played. He holds the NHL record for most consecutive seasons with 20 or more goals. He did it 22 years in a row. He has led the NHL playoffs in scoring for six different playoff runs, another record. Finally, he has 23 NHL All-Star appearances, which is the most all-time.

There are more records, but for brevity, Gordie Howe's incredible career was more than worthy of the "Mr. Hockey" moniker he earned over those years on the ice. He played the game with tenacity and skill, a combination rarely seen in today's game. He was a special player, and his stamp on the game is likely to be eternal.

## Did You Know?

1. Howe was named to the All-Star game 23 times.

2. He ranks second in all-time NHL games played with 1,767.

3. Howe's participation in the WHA helped the leagues merge in the 1970s.

4. He received the first Lifetime Achievement Award in 2008.

5. Howe was ambidextrous, meaning he could play left- or right-handed with a straight blade on his stick.

6. Howe once appeared on the TV game show *To Tell the Truth*, in 1967.

# CHAPTER 18:

## DOMINIK HASEK

Over the decades of NHL competition, the position of goaltender has evolved to compete with the growing skill and speed of offensive players. Goalies study different styles and use their strong technical skills to make more saves, at least statistically. They play the game that will make the most saves, on average. However, every once in a great while, an NHL goaltender will ignore much of what they have learned in an act of desperation, diving and flailing to keep the puck from crossing the line.

When most hockey fans think of this kind of desperation save, the name that often comes to mind is Dominik Hasek. His career is full of incredible saves that few would have considered possible. And yet, the "Dominator" seemingly always found the save he needed to make.

Let's examine the spectacular career of one of the most unorthodox goaltenders to ever play in the NHL.

Dominik Hasek began playing at five, and he fell in love with the game immediately. He was a natural in goal, and he worked on his skills as he grew. At age 16, he became the youngest player to ever play at the professional level. One year later, though, he was drafted by his country's army, and he played a season with an army team.

Then, he played for his national team at the 1982 World Junior Championships, where his team earned silver medals. As this tournament took place in the United States,

NHL scouts got a good look at Hasek. The next summer, during the 1983 draft, Hasek was selected as the 199th overall pick by the Chicago Blackhawks.

Though he was selected by an NHL team, it would still be several years before he made the trip across the ocean to play in North America. He continued to excel in the Extraliga, the professional league in Czechoslovakia, where he won the Golden Hockey Stick three times in four seasons. It was the award given to the MVP of the league, and Hasek had dominated almost nonstop for half a decade.

Finally, in the fall of 1990, Hasek played his first season in the NHL. He served as the backup to Eddie Belfour, which meant he didn't get much time on the ice. Belfour was an established, elite goaltender, so Hasek was only named the starter for 25 games over two seasons.

One of his appearances came during the team's Stanley Cup Finals defeat to the Pittsburgh Penguins, but he played well in relief of Belfour, which attracted the attention of his next team, the Buffalo Sabres. During the 1992–93 season, Hasek was the backup to Grant Fuhr in Buffalo until Fuhr suffered an injury. Hasek then became the starter, and he took the opportunity.

Over the next eight and a half seasons, Hasek demonstrated his skill and knack for fancy saves, as he would often throw away his goal stick to get his blocker in front of the puck faster. He also showed how well he could track the puck and use any part of his body to make a save. One particular save came against the Montreal Canadiens when a pass came across the front of the net.

Hasek stretched out his left leg to make the pad save along the ice, but the rebound went right to another Montreal player who shot the puck immediately, trying to lift it over Hasek's pad and into the open net. Hasek, at the last moment, lifted his left skate off the ice, his leg bent at the knee that was still on the ice, to save the rebound.

It was a spectacular save, but it was just one of many highlight-reel stops from the Dominator.

Another go-to desperation move of Dominik's was the windmill, where he would lay down on his back and fan out his pads in a motion that looks like a windshield wiper moving from one side to the other, following the attacking player as he moves across the front of the net with the puck. If a windmill was not necessary, sometimes Hasek would just lie on his back and throw his arms out, covering as much of the lower part of the net as possible.

Hasek played well in Buffalo, but after a heartbreaking loss in the Stanley Cup Finals against the Dallas Stars and two more seasons of playoff disappointments, he was traded to the Detroit Red Wings for another chance at a championship. In Detroit, he helped the team through the regular season with a career-high 41 regular season wins and a .915 save percentage. The team won the Presidents' Trophy with the best record in the league, aided by Hasek and several other future Hall-of-Fame players on the roster.

However, when Hasek and the Wings began their playoff run, they ran into trouble immediately. In the first round against the Vancouver Canucks, Detroit lost Game 1 in overtime, as Hasek allowed four goals on 26 shots. Then, they were beaten 5-2 in Game 2, with Hasek only making 15 saves on 19 shots. With two home losses already in the series, many considered the run to be over before it started.

Hasek and the Wings found a way to bounce back, though. In Game 3, he stopped 22 of 23 shots and the Wings won 3-1. Two nights later, he stopped 22 of 24, helping Detroit to a 4-2 victory, evening the series. In Game 5, Hasek was a perfect 25 for 25. He did give up four goals on 29 shots in Game 6, but Detroit found enough offense to overcome the Canucks and win the series.

The second round against the St. Louis Blues featured another hiccup for Hasek and the team, as he gave up five goals in Game 3. However, it was Detroit's only loss in the round, and Hasek had shutouts in Games 1 and 5 to win the series in five games.

In the Western Conference Finals, Hasek had to experience more of the rivalry between Detroit and Colorado. In an intense series between the two teams, the Red Wings found themselves behind after losing Game 5 in overtime, 2-1. Colorado had a 3-2 series lead, with a chance to advance to the Stanley Cup Finals with one more victory.

Hasek was determined to win his first Stanley Cup, though, so he and Detroit buckled down. In Games 6 and 7, Colorado did not score. The Wings won Game 6 by a score of 2-0, and Game 7 was a 7-0 romp. Hasek made 43 saves between the two games for Detroit.

In the Finals, Hasek continued his great play, and although Detroit fell in overtime to open the series, they would go on to win the next four straight and claim the Stanley Cup. Game 4 was a shutout for Hasek, and he only allowed a total of seven goals over those five games. It was the one piece of a legendary career that Hasek still needed, and he finally got it at the age of 37.

He would play another partial season with Detroit before heading to Ottawa. He played 43 games with the Senators before heading back to Detroit. He played two more seasons with the Wings, including another Cup run in 2008. However, Hasek did not feature in the playoffs, as he was pulled during the first round in favor of Chris Osgood.

With two Stanley Cup Rings at the age of 43, Hasek headed back overseas to finish his career in the Czech Republic and Russian hockey leagues.

On the page, it probably seems ridiculous that a goaltender with such low-percentage antics would ever be successful playing at the highest level of hockey in the world, but Dominik Hasek made it work. During his professional career, Hasek amassed many awards and records. He is tied for first among retired goaltenders in career save percentage with a .922.

He is also tied for the most shutouts in a month, as he notched six of them during the 1997–98 season. Most impressively, he holds the NHL record for most saves in a shutout when he stopped 70 shots for the Sabres during their playoff series against the New Jersey Devils.

Dominik Hasek played the game of hockey much differently than most goalies do. He used every tool available to him, even if his save attempts did not look like the best option at that moment. This created incredible moments in the crease, making Hasek an entertaining goalie for his team, even if his antics raised the blood pressure of his teammates and the fans in attendance. He was an incredible player who left a unique mark on the game.

## Did You Know?

1. Wayne Gretzky once called Hasek "the best player in the game."

2. His 'goals against' average ranks seventh all-time, but first in the modern era.

3. Hasek is the only goaltender to ever face the most shots per 60 minutes and also finish first in save percentage in a season.

4. When Hasek retired at 43, he was the second-oldest active player in the league.

5. Some called Hasek's unorthodox style "flopping" because he would fall to the ice for almost every shot on goal.

6. Hasek is only 11th on the all-time list for wins, at 389.

# CHAPTER 19:

## BRETT HULL'S CUP-WINNING GOAL?

The question mark in the title of this chapter is not there by error. The 1999 Stanley Cup Finals was an intense matchup between the Dallas Stars and the Buffalo Sabres. The series was closely contested throughout, with each team winning games and fighting for the chance to raise the Stanley Cup. Unfortunately for one team, and hockey fans everywhere, this series ended in the most incredible, yet controversial, fashion.

Let's examine the 1999 Stanley Cup Finals finale and why it was such a big deal.

First, the teams.

The Dallas Stars of this era had several future Hall of Fame players on the roster, including goaltender Ed Belfour and forwards Mike Modano, Guy Carbonneau, Joe Nieuwendyk, and Brett Hull. On the other side, they obviously had a good squad, but the only Hall of Fame-bound player was their goalie, Dominik Hasek.

Now, going into the series, the Dallas Stars were the favorites to win. At the end of the regular season, the Stars were the top seed in the league, as they won the Presidents' Trophy for the best record. The next closest team was nine points back. As for the Sabres, they made the playoffs by a comfortable margin, but they were the seventh seed out of eight in the Eastern Conference.

Still, both teams had impressive runs to reach the Finals. The Sabres swept the second-seeded Ottawa Senators in the first round, and the Stars also swept the Edmonton Oilers in their opening series. Dallas defeated St. Louis in the second round, needing six games to do so, and the Sabres also needed six games to overcome the Boston Bruins. In the Conference Finals, Dallas went the distance with a strong Colorado team, while Buffalo was able to handle the Toronto Maple Leafs in five games.

Because Buffalo had played fewer games, they were considered more rested for the Finals, though that does not mean too much for athletes of their caliber. Regardless, Buffalo struck first in the Finals, winning Game 1 in overtime. Dallas responded with wins in Games 2 and 3, but Buffalo tied the series once more with a win in Game 4.

Game 5 went to Dallas, giving them a chance to win the Stanley Cup with a victory in Game 6. This game, Game 6 of the 1999 Stanley Cup Finals, ended in such a way that it left players and fans talking about it for a long time. Some of the people involved in the game might still have bitter feelings about it.

The game was much like those that preceded it, as it was closely played and low-scoring. The Stars scored in the first period, while the Sabres struck late in the second period to tie the score at one. What followed was a scoreless third period, sending the game to overtime.

The overtime period came and went, with neither team being able to find the back of the net. The pressure was growing as each team wanted victory. Buffalo wanted to extend the series and win the Cup for themselves in Game 7, while Dallas wanted to get the job done immediately. Players from both teams were anxious to win their first championship.

Both goaltenders wanted to hoist the trophy over their heads, an experience that had escaped both to this point in their careers. Belfour and Hasek, coincidentally, had both been in the Stanley Cup Finals once before. Belfour was the starting goaltender for the Chicago Blackhawks when they reached the series in 1992, and Hasek was his backup.

The second overtime period continued, and both eager goaltenders kept the puck from getting by, frustrating their opponents as everyone on the ice continued to tire out from the extra time on the ice.

Brett Hull, the player who would unintentionally cause the controversial ending to this game, was also looking to capture his first Stanley Cup in his second visit to the Finals. For him, though, it had been several years since his last appearance. He was a member of the Calgary Flames when they lost to the Montreal Canadiens in the 1986 Finals.

The game stretched into a third overtime, and both players and spectators began to understand that however this game ended, it would be monumental. Rarely do games in the Stanley Cup Finals last as long as this one had.

Finally, with 5:09 left in the third overtime, Brett Hull found himself with a chance in close. As the puck skipped toward the net, Hull tried to deflect it toward Hasek, who made the save with his paddle. Hull tried to find the rebound as Hasek went to his stomach and stretched out his arms to cover the puck and end the play. However, Hull found the puck at the edge of the crease as a Buffalo defender tried to check him away. That defender missed, and Hull turned with the puck on his skate, pulling it to his stick and leaving him with an open upper half of the goal to fire the puck into and celebrate the Stanley Cup victory.

As the Stars celebrated, an overhead replay of the goal was shown on the big screens in the arena, prompting the Buffalo players and coaches to begin asking if the goal had been legal. On the replay, Brett Hull's skate was clearly in Dominik Hasek's goal crease as he fought to gain possession of the puck and put it in the net. There were heated arguments from the Buffalo coaching staff that night, but the NHL ruled that the goal was good, because Hull's skate bringing the puck out of the crease counted as possession of the puck, meaning that Hull could be in the crease to take the shot.

The Dallas Stars had captured their first Stanley Cup, becoming the first team from the southern half of the United States to win the title!

To this day, Buffalo Sabres fans refer to this play as "No goal," because they still believe that Hull was illegally in the crease at the moment of the play and that the puck being against his skate did not count as possession of the puck.

Because of this situation, the NHL decided to change the rule soon after, meaning that players could be on or in the crease to play the puck, as long as they did not interfere with the goaltender's ability to make a play on the puck. This meant that players would no longer have to slam on the brakes in fear of one of their toes crossing that line while their teammate scored on the other side of the net.

Lots of frustration stemmed from that rule, and it culminated in the 1999 Stanley Cup Finals, where one beleaguered franchise is still waiting for its first Stanley Cup Championship. The city of Buffalo suffers cruelty from many of its professional sports teams, but this incredible play is one of the most painful, considering how close they were to the ultimate prize. Here's hoping they get to the top one day soon.

## Did You Know?

1. The Stars had three players who were on their fourth trip to the Finals (Skrudland, Keane, and Carbonneau).

2. The Stars returned to the Finals the next year to defend their title, but they lost to the Devils in six games.

3. This was the first series since 1994 that took more than four games to decide.

4. Joe Nieuwendyk was named MVP of the Finals.

5. The series also had fighting majors for the first time in three years.

6. Mike Modano broke his wrist in Game 2, and Hull suffered a minor groin injury in Game 3.

# CONCLUSION

You've reached the end of this book, after 19 incredible stories that span decades of hockey history, much like the storied career of Gordie Howe. You've read the tales of some of the more epic games that stretched into multiple overtimes and tested the body and will of all who had to go through it. There were chapters dedicated to the trailblazing women who helped the game grow exponentially for those who had been excluded for far too long.

The hope is that the stories in these pages illustrate how special this sport can be when it is played with respect and dignity. Players put everything they have on the line for their teammates, and the fans are blessed with the opportunity to see the incredible moments night in and night out.

There are tons of incredible hockey players, moments, and games not covered in this book because it is impossible to tell all of the most incredible hockey stories to ever happen. Hopefully, though, the stories presented here will inspire the hockey fan in you to explore more of the history behind the game. Players have been chasing that little rubber puck for over a century now, meaning that thousands of players have gone through the leagues and tournaments held all around the world.

If you enjoyed this book, consider passing it along to a friend. The game of hockey can be difficult for potential fans, as the speed of the game is intimidating for those watching the action for the first time. The best part of this book, though, is that you experienced all of these incredible stories at your own reading pace!

The game of hockey is a beautiful one, full of skill and speed, brutal strength, and the occasional mind games between player and goaltender. Each one of these battles taking place over a cold sheet of frozen, rock-solid ice only adds to the stakes. The NHL used to say that hockey was the "Coolest game on earth," a nod to that frozen surface. While the temperature inside the arenas can be quite cold, it is easier to say that hockey is the most incredible sport ever played.

Made in United States
Orlando, FL
13 December 2024

55583046R00089